PHOTO FINISHES

GREAT LAST-SECOND, BOTTOM-OF-THE-NINTH, SUDDEN-DEATH VICTORIES

MICHAEL E. GOODMAN

A *Sports Illustrated For Kids* Book

For Brett, who brings sports alive
in our house every season and who
always makes us cheer.

Book design by Signet M. Design, Inc.

Library of Congress Cataloging-in-Publication Data

Goodman, Michael E.
    Photo finishes : great last second, bottom of the ninth, sudden
death victories / by Michael E. Goodman.—1st ed.
      p. cm.
    "A Sports Illustrated for kids book."
    Summary: Presents true sports stories of victory snatched from the
jaws of defeat.
    ISBN 0-316-32023-4
    1. Sports—Juvenile literature.   [1. Sports—Miscellanea.]
I. Title
GV707.G56   1990   89-48065
796—dc20   CIP
                                                             AC

SPORTS ILLUSTRATED FOR KIDS is a trademark of THE TIME INC. MAGAZINE COMPANY.

Sports Illustrated For Kids Books is a joint imprint of Little, Brown and Company and Warner Juvenile Books. This title is published in arrangement with Cloverdale Press Inc.

10 9 8 7 6 5 4 3 2 1

RRD OH

For further information regarding this title, write to Little, Brown and Company, 34 Beacon Street, Boston, MA 02108

Published simultaneously in Canada by Little, Brown & Company (Canada) Limited

Printed in the United States of America

CONTENTS

*H*AVE YOU EVER HAD THIS DREAM? YOUR baseball team is behind by a run in the seventh game of the World Series. There are two outs in the bottom of the ninth. One of your teammates is on first base, and you're at bat. The fans are standing and cheering. Here comes the pitch. It's a high, hard one—just the kind you like. You swing with all your might, and *boom!* It's going, going, gone. A home run!

Or how about this dream? There are five seconds left in the national basketball championship game. Your team is behind by a point. You bring the ball upcourt, keeping one eye on the clock. Four... three... there isn't enough time to pass off or drive to the basket. You have to shoot from 15 feet out. The ball hits the rim, bounces high above the basket... and then falls right through for the winning points. Your team wins the game, and you're the hero!

Then you wake up, and you realize that it was only a dream. For a few lucky athletes those kinds of dreams have actually come true. For instance in 1960 Bill Mazeroski of the Pittsburgh Pirates hit a home run in the bottom of the ninth inning of the seventh game of the World Series. That shot beat the New York Yankees and made the Pirates world champs.

Bottom-of-the-ninth home runs, last-second touchdowns, overtime hockey goals, buzzer-beating basketball shots—those events make the magic moments in sports history. So do the victories that are created by almost super-human efforts by great athletes, as well as some lucky bounces or referees' mistakes that lead to last-second wins.

You can read about lots of exciting sports stories with dramatic endings just by turning the page in this book. So Bobby Thomson is coming to bat. His team is behind by two runs. Two runners are on base, and it's the bottom of the ninth.... ★

HIGH DRAMA

The Suns vs. the Celtics.

You have probably watched a game that came down to the last play or to the last three seconds. If you're lucky, maybe you have even played in one! Either way you know what it's like. Your hands feel sweaty, your heart races, you breathe quickly. What's going to happen? Who's going to win? ★

Bobby Thomson connects on Ralph Branca's inside fastball for his game-winning three-run homer.

THE SHOT HEARD ROUND THE WORLD

THE DATE WAS OCTOBER 3, 1951. BOBBY Thomson of the New York Giants stepped up to bat. The Brooklyn Dodgers were leading the Giants, 4–2, in the bottom of the ninth. This was the third game of a special three-game playoff series between the two teams that had tied for the National League pennant. The winner would head to the World Series. The loser would . . . . Nobody wanted to think about losing.

Pinch runner Clint Hartung took a lead off third base, and Whitey Lockman did the same off second. Dodger manager Chuck Dressen called on a relief pitcher, Ralph Branca. Branca knew his job. It was to get the Giants next hitter, third baseman Bobby Thomson, to make an out. Once Branca retired Thomson, he could concentrate on Willie Mays, who followed Thomson in the Giants lineup. Three outs, and the Dodgers would finally end the dreams of the upstart Giants.

Those dreams had begun two months before. In early August nobody thought the Giants would win the pennant. Brooklyn was 13½ games ahead of New York, and most people thought the Dodgers would breeze to the pennant. Giants fans weren't happy with that idea. They never liked it when their team lost, but they hated it when the Giants lost to the Dodgers. The two teams were fierce rivals because they played in the same city. (Brooklyn is part of New York City.)

The Brooklyn players and rooters were no doubt feeling pretty confident in early August of 1951. The Giants, however, didn't seem to feel that things were hopeless yet. They made a few changes on the field. Manager Leo Durocher wanted to get his star rookie, Willie Mays, into the lineup, so he put outfielder Bobby Thomson at third base and sent Mays to centerfield. Mays gave the Giants great fielding in center and some strong hitting, too. And all of a sudden Thomson's bat got hot. He batted almost .350 the rest of the season and wound up with 32 home runs and 101 runs batted in. It was Thomson's finest year ever.

The Giants began to win and cut into Brooklyn's lead. At first, Dodger fans weren't concerned. They didn't even worry when the Giants swept a three-game series from their heroes in mid-August. It was no big deal. The lead was still 9 1/2 games. Then the Dodgers won 10 out of 16 games. But the Giants won 16 straight! Suddenly it looked as if there was going to be a pennant race after all. The Giants were closing in on their rivals.

With two weeks left in the season, Brooklyn was up by 4 1/2 games. But the Dodgers could feel the Giants breathing down their necks. With only two games left in the season, the Dodgers 13-game lead was down to zero.

Both the Dodgers and Giants won their last two games to finish in a tie. That meant the Dodgers and Giants would have to compete in a best-two-of-three playoff to decide the pennant winner. The Giants had won an amazing 37 of their last 44 games, but they still had to win 2 more to make it to the World Series.

Ebbets Field, the Dodgers stadium, was packed and rocking on October 1 for the first game of the playoffs. Almost every New Yorker who couldn't get into the stadium was listening on the radio. After all, this was more than just a battle for the National League pennant—it was the Dodgers versus the Giants, New York City's biggest rivals!

The Giants won the first game, 3–1, after Bobby Thomson hit a home run off Dodger reliever Ralph Branca. It was unbelievable, but the Giants were just one win away from the pennant! The Dodgers weren't giving up, however. The next day they walloped New York, 10–0, to even up the series.

Each team had its ace pitcher ready to go in the third game. Sal Maglie was on the mound for the Giants. His nickname was "The Barber" because he liked to throw the ball inside to batters and give them a "close shave." Don Newcombe was pitching for the Dodgers. He had won 20 games during the season.

Brooklyn scored a run in the first

inning to take a 1–0 lead. New York had some trouble with Newcombe, however. The big Dodger righthander held them to just two hits and no runs through the first six innings.

In the bottom of the seventh, the Giants put together a double by Monte Irvin, a sacrifice hit by Whitey Lockman and a long fly ball by Bobby Thomson to tie the score. But Brooklyn came right back with a three-run eighth inning to move in front again, 4–1. Newcombe struck out three Giants batters in the bottom of the eighth to hold New York in check. Now the Giants were down to their last three outs.

Before the ninth inning began, Newcombe told manager Charlie Dressen, "It looks like I don't have it any more, Skipper. You'd better take me out." Dressen didn't agree. Because Newcombe had pitched well in the eighth and his teammates were counting on him, he decided to send "Newk" back to the mound.

As the Giants came up to bat their manager, Leo Durocher, told them, "We've gone this far. Let's give them a finish." And what a finish it was!

Giants shortstop Alvin Dark got an infield hit to open the bottom of the ninth. Don Mueller followed with a single. With runners now at first and third, Newcombe got Monte Irvin to hit a foul pop-up for the first out. Whitey Lockman was the next hitter. He wanted to poke an inside pitch

into the rightfield stands to tie the game, but Newcombe kept the ball outside. So Lockman slapped an outside pitch into leftfield for a double. That scored one run and put Mueller on third and Lockman on second. Lockman represented the tying run. Clint Hartung came in to run for Mueller, who had hurt his ankle sliding into third.

Dressen decided to replace his pitcher at the same time. He called on Branca to save the game and the pennant.

Up stepped Bobby Thomson. Remember, when Thomson faced Branca in Game 1, Thomson had hit a game-winning home run. Also the last time Thomson was up in Game 3, he had hit a long fly ball to even the score. Branca wanted to make sure that things would go the Dodgers' way this time. His first pitch to Thomson was a called strike. Hoping to tie up Thomson, the Dodger pitcher decided to put the next one over high and tight. The pitch went just where Branca wanted it to go. For a split second the Dodger pitcher probably thought about where he would throw the next pitch in order to strike out Thomson. But only for a split second.

Thomson stepped back from the plate to hit the inside pitch. He took a powerful swing and connected. The ball went like a rocket into the leftfield bleachers only a short distance

Thomson is mobbed by his teammates—and some excited fans—after touching home plate.

away. Suddenly the score was 5–4 Giants, and the game was over!

New York radio announcer Russ Hodges began yelling over the air, "The Giants win the pennant! The Giants win the pennant! The Giants win the pennant! They're going crazy! They are going crazy! Ooooh, boy!" The Dodgers stood stunned on the field, then slowly and sadly walked back to their dugout. Branca lay face-down on the dugout steps and did not talk or move for several minutes.

Bobby Thomson's bottom-of-the-ninth home run made him an instant hero. That blast was later given several nicknames. It was called "The Shot Heard 'Round the World." Even American soldiers fighting halfway around the world in Korea heard about the home run. Some people also named it "The Miracle at Coogan's Bluff" (named after the place where the Polo Grounds field was located). The real miracle, however, was that the Giants had come back to tie the Dodgers during the season to force the playoff.

Most of all Bobby Thomson's homer was an athlete's dream come true. ★

No Joy in Beantown

OST BASEBALL FANS AGREED: THERE COULD never be a comeback as thrilling or as unbelievable as that of the New York Giants in 1951. And there could never be a home run as dramatic as Bobby Thomson's.

Then in 1978 the two biggest rivals in the American League began almost an "instant replay" of 1951. The two teams were the Boston Red Sox and the New York Yankees.

Like the Giants and Dodgers, the Red Sox and Yankees really didn't like each other very much. And their fans didn't have a single nice word to say about the other team. The dislike went back a long way—at least to 1919. In that year, Red Sox owner Harry Frazee was having some money problems. In return for $125,000 and a loan from Yankees owner Jacob Ruppert, he gave up a strong, young lefthanded pitcher named Babe Ruth, who was also a pretty good hitter. Ruth had helped lead the Sox to the American League title in 1915 and to World Series wins in 1916 and 1918.

he Yankees owner agreed to purchase the Babe's contract. What a deal that turned out to be! Ruth, who went on to become the greatest slugger and most popular player in baseball history, turned the Yankees into winners. Ruth played in New York for 15 years. In that time the Yanks won seven pennants and four world championships, and they kept winning even after Ruth retired. Boston didn't win another pennant for 27 years. Boston fans never forgave their owner for letting the Babe get away, and they hated the Yankees for "stealing" their treasure.

You can imagine then, how happy the Red Sox fans were when they looked at the American League Eastern Division standings on July 19, 1978. Their team, led by Carl Yastrzemski, Carlton Fisk, Fred Lynn, Jim Rice and Dwight Evans, was in first place. The hated Yankees were in fourth place—14 games back! The Yankees were even fighting with each other. Star player Reggie Jackson and manager Billy Martin could not get along. Finally Martin was fired on July 23. Just before Martin left, however, his team began a five-game winning streak while Boston was losing four straight. When Bob Lemon took over as new manager on July 25, the Yankees were "just" 10$\frac{1}{2}$ games back. Red Sox fans still weren't worried, but they should have been.

Lemon made a few changes, and New York kept winning. When Boston went to New York on August 2 for 2 games, the lead was 6$\frac{1}{2}$ games. New Yorkers were ready for their team to close the gap with the Red Sox even further. The Yankees broke out to a 5–0 lead in the first first game, but the Sox came back to tie. The game was still tied in the 14th inning when it had to be stopped due to an American League rule that said no inning could begin after 1:00 A.M.

The game continued the next night. Boston scored two runs in the 17th inning for the win. Then the Sox won the second game, and their lead over the Yankees was back to 8$\frac{1}{2}$ games.

On September 7 the Yankees went to Boston for a four-game series. The two teams were now just four games apart. Everybody knew that this series in Fenway Park would decide who would win the division title. Those games have gone down in baseball history as "The Boston Massacre." Playing in front of huge crowds in Fenway, the Red Sox couldn't do anything right...and the Yankees couldn't do anything wrong. New York crushed Boston in all four games: 15–3, 13–2, 7–0 and 7–4. The two teams were tied for first place!

In the next few days the Yanks moved ahead of Boston. The teams

squared off the next week in Yankee Stadium. New York won 2 of 3 and opened up a $2^1/_2$ game lead with 14 games left in the season.

The Red Sox didn't give up, however. In the next week the Sox moved within one game of the Yankees. There were only seven games to go. Boston won six in a row—and so did New York. All of a sudden the entire season was down to the last game. If the Red Sox lost to Toronto or the Yankees beat Cleveland, it would be all over. Boston won its game, 5–0. The Red Sox players and fans waited for news from New York. It was terrific news! Cleveland's Rick Waits pitched a great game to defeat the

Yankees 9–2, and the division race was tied once again. The scoreboard in Fenway Park spelled it out in big letters: "THANK YOU RICK WAITS!"

The next day Boston fans began preparing for a one-game playoff against the Yankees. Mike Torrez, who had played for the Yankees in 1977, would be pitching for Boston. The fans thought nothing would be sweeter than for a former Yankee's player to shut down New York's pennant hopes. Torrez's opponent would be Ron Guidry, who had an amazing 24–3 record for the season.

Every seat in Fenway Park was occupied on October 2, 1978. Nearly every television set in Boston and New York—and most of the rest of the country—was tuned to the game. Long-time Sox star Carl Yastrzemski, who was known as "Yaz," put Boston ahead 1–0 with a tremendous home run in the second inning. The lead went to 2–0 in the sixth. Red Sox fans were going crazy!

Meanwhile the Yankees couldn't do anything against Torrez. They squeaked out only two hits in the first six innings. Just before the seventh inning began, Yankees outfielder Paul Blair told his teammates, "This is going to be our inning. I think we're going to score four runs." Was Blair just hoping, or did he have ESP?

In any case Yankees third baseman Graig Nettles must not have been listening, because he opened the inning with a fly ball to rightfield for the first out. Then Roy White and Chris Chambliss hit back-to-back singles to start a Yankees rally. Jim Spencer came up as a pinch hitter for the Yanks. Although Spencer was a left-handed hitter, he had good power to leftfield. And Fenway Park's leftfield wall, known as "The Green Monster," was only 315 feet away. If Torrez made a mistake with Spencer, the Yankees could take the lead. Torrez made no mistakes. Spencer sent an easy fly to Yaz in leftfield for the second out.

That brought up weak-hitting shortstop, Bucky Dent, who had hit only four home runs all year. Nobody expected him to put on a power display. Dent took the first pitch for a ball, he fouled the second pitch off his left ankle. The pitch not only hurt Dent's ankle, it also broke his bat. When the Yankees batboy brought out a new one, he made a serious mistake. The batboy brought Dent one of Mickey Rivers' bats.

On the next pitch Dent sent a high fly ball toward The Green Monster. Standing at the base of the wall, Yaz waited for the ball to come down. It never did. Dent's shot landed in the screen on top of the wall. The Yankees—the hated Yankees—were ahead! New York added one more run to take a 4–2 lead, just as Paul

Blair had predicted.

In the top of the eighth inning Reggie Jackson hit a 420-foot home run to put New York up 5–2. Red Sox fans were pretty down. However, they got a lift in the bottom of the eighth. After Boston second baseman Jerry Remy hit a double, Yaz singled him home to make the score 5–3. Two more singles closed the gap to 5–4 before the inning ended.

Boston had one more chance in the ninth inning. With one out and a runner on first, Remy hit a shot to rightfield. Yankee rightfielder "Sweet" Lou Piniella lost the ball in the sun and didn't know where it was going. Yet when Lou stuck his glove out, the ball bounced into it! Although Piniella pretended that this was only a routine play, everyone watching the game knew it was a miracle. If the ball had gotten past him, it would have been a triple for the speedy Remy. The score would have been tied, and Boston would have had the winning run on third base with only one out and the team's two best hitters coming up next. Instead it was a single, and runners stood on first and second, and the Yankees were still leading.

Jim Rice was up next—just the man Sox fans would have ordered. Voted the league's Most Valuable Player in 1978 with 46 homers and 139 runs batted in, the Boston slugger sent a shot to deep right. Fans stood on their tiptoes, straining—and hoping—to see it go out of the park. But Piniella grabbed it near the wall for out Number 2.

The Red Sox had one final chance to come back and win the game, and that chance belonged to Carl Yastrzemski. A future Hall of Famer, Yaz became the only man in baseball history to record more than 3,000 hits and 400 home runs in his career. Even before their hero stepped into the batter's box, Boston fans began cheering, and they kept cheering when he took ball one from Yankees relief pitcher "Goose" Gossage. When Gossage challenged Yaz with a 95-mile-per-hour fastball, the cheering turned to groans as Yastrzemski sent a soft foul fly to Graig Nettles at third base. Nettles caught the ball; the game—and Boston's hope for a pennant—was over.

In 1978 the Yankees went on to defeat the Kansas City Royals for the American League pennant and the Los Angeles Dodgers for the World Championship. The Red Sox and their fans went home to think sadly about what might have been. If only Mike Torrez hadn't served up that fat pitch to Bucky Dent.... If only Lou Piniella hadn't made that miracle catch.... If only Rice or Yaz had come through.... If only Harry Frazee hadn't sold Babe Ruth's contract to the Yankees in 1919.... If only... ★

THE TIE

ICTURE THIS. THERE IS LESS THAN A MINUTE left in a college football game between the two oldest rivals in American sports. Neither team has lost a game all season. The stadium is so crowded that it is bursting at the seams; one team is ahead by 16 points. From the outset the fans are celebrating and making fun of the rival team's fans. They shout, "You're Number Two!" The other team is being led by its second-string quarterback who has seen very little action all year.

The scene was Harvard Stadium in Cambridge, Massachusetts, on November 23, 1968. The event was "The Game."

The New York Giants and the Brooklyn Dodgers were fierce rivals. The Red Sox and the Yankees still are. But there is no older sports rivalry in this country than Harvard versus Yale in college football. For one thing, those two schools invented most of the rules of football. They played their first game against each other in 1875. In those days the football was round, passing wasn't allowed and players didn't wear pads or helmets. In those days the Harvard–Yale game usually decided which was the best team in the country. That's why the contest between the two teams became known simply as "The Game." To many people, it was the only game that mattered. In 1968 "The Game" was something special. For the first time in 50 years, both teams came into it undefeated.

The Harvard Crimson had a solid offense, led by halfback and team captain Vic Gatto. But it was the Crimson defense that made the team so unbeatable— Harvard's was the best in the Ivy League. On the other hand, The Yale Elis (pronounced E-lies) drew its strength from its offense. Ranked Number 1 in the East, the Elis were among the top 20 teams in America. Heading up the Yale offense were quarterback Brian Dowling and halfback Calvin Hill, who went on to the National Football League after they graduated. So the best defensive team in the league was up against the best offensive team. That was the perfect combination for a great football game.

There had never been such a build up for an Ivy League game. The game started out slowly, however. For the first 25 minutes of play, Yale was completely in charge. The Elis were ahead 22–0. The Harvard fans spirits didn't improve much when Harvard coach John Yovicsin decided to try a desperate move. He sent in second-string quarterback Frank Chiampi. Chiampi was a very strong passer. Still, although he could throw a football more than 80 yards in the air, he didn't have much experience. His presence on the field created quite a stir among his teammates.

Chiampi went to work just before halftime. Having led the Crimson quickly down the field, he completed a 15-yard touchdown pass with 39 seconds to go in the half. That brought the Crimson a little closer at 22–6. Harvard decided to pass for the extra point instead of kick. Under college rules, a team gets two points for a successful run or pass after it scores a touchdown. But Chiampi had trouble handling the snap from center, and the busted play cost the Crimson the opportunity to put more points on the board.

Things started to turn Harvard's way at the beginning of the third quarter, when the Elis made the first of a series of errors. The Yale punt returner fumbled a Harvard kick, and the Crimson recovered the ball on the Elis' 25-yard line. Harvard then scored three plays to pull within 9 points, at 22–13.

At the start of the final quarter Yale came back with a drive of its own. Dowling took the ball in for the touchdown to increase the lead to 28–13. Yale coach Carmen Cozza then made a decision he would soon regret. Rather than go for a two-point conversion, he decided to kick the extra point. The kick was good, and Yale led by 16 points. There were just under 11 minutes left in the game.

Yale began another drive. Some Yale fans felt that Dowling should have tried to use up the clock by keeping the ball on the ground. The

Yale quarterback kept passing. He wanted one more touchdown to seal the victory. With over three minutes remaining in the game the Elis were driving toward the Crimson goal yet again. Waving white handkerchiefs at the Harvard side of the field, Yale fans began yelling, "You're Number Two!"

Suddenly a loud cheer went up on the Harvard side. Trying to pick up a few extra yards Yale fullback Bob Levin had fumbled the ball and Harvard recovered deep in its own territory. Chiampi ran onto the field. In a little over two minutes, Chiampi directed his team to a touchdown. That made the score 29–19 with 42 seconds left to play.

Harvard fans started imagining some wild possibilities. If the Crimson could make a 2-point conversion, the team would be just 8 points behind. If Harvard could recover a Yale fumble on the kickoff, drive for another touchdown and make another 2-point conversion—all in less than 42 seconds—the game would be tied.

The plan depended on one thing. The Crimson had to make a two-point conversion. Chiampi went back to pass, the Elis put on a big rush, and Chiampi had to get off the pass faster than he wanted to. It fell incomplete: That meant the game was definitely lost. But wait a minute! A referee had thrown a penalty flag on the play. A Yale defensive player was called for pass interference. Harvard got the chance to run another play, and this time the pass was completed. The score was 29–21.

On the kickoff, the Harvard kicker sent a line drive at one of the Yale players standing up front to block on the kickoff. The ball bounced off the Yale player, and Harvard recovered it on the 49-yard line—everything was going according to plan. The Crimson had just under 40 seconds to make it into the end zone.

On the next play Chiampi went back to pass. When he couldn't find an open receiver, he began to run with the ball. He raced 14 yards and then tried to get out of bounds to stop the clock. A Yale player tackled Chiampi around his helmet. If the defender had grabbed the faceguard on the front of Chiampi's helmet, that would be a big 15-yard penalty. Although the Yale player was certain he had not grabbled the faceguard, the referee disagreed and called the penalty. That moved the ball to the Yale 20-yard line.

By now fans on both sides of the field were standing on their feet and screaming. The Harvard fans were yelling encouragement to their team. The Yale fans couldn't *believe* what had happened to their 22-point lead.

A few plays later Harvard faced

fourth down. Time was running out. A Yale defender grabbed the Crimson quarterback behind the line and was about to tackle him in what looked like the last play of the game. Suddenly another miracle occurred. Chiampi fumbled or pushed or rolled the ball forward. (There is still some debate about just what happened.) A Harvard lineman fell on the loose ball on the Yale eight-yard line. It was a Harvard first down. Three seconds remained in the game!

Everyone in the stadium knew the next play was going to be a pass into the end zone. Chiampi took the hike. He went back, rolled to one side, then to the other side. Time seemed to have stopped. Finally Chiampi spotted Vic Gatto open in the end zone. He let loose and—touchdown! The Harvard fans erupted with joy. Yale fans, who had been waving their handkerchiefs moments before, now used them to wipe the tears from their eyes. The scoreboard read: Yale 29–Harvard 27. The clock read: 0:00.

Since the rules of football dictate that a team gets to try for the extra point even if there's no time left on the clock, the whole game and the whole season came down to one play. Once more Chiampi went back to pass, looking to make the two-point conversion. Hoping that someone would get open, he ran from side

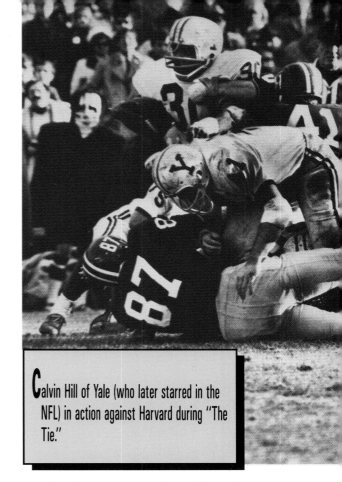

Calvin Hill of Yale (who later starred in the NFL) in action against Harvard during "The Tie."

to side. The Crimson's big tight end, Pete Varney, began waving his arms in the corner of the end zone. Behind him, blocked from view, was Eli defender Ed Franklin. Chiampi threw a bullet toward Varney. Franklin crashed into the receiver, but he was too late. Hugging the ball to his chest, Varney began jumping up and down with excitement. Harvard had done it! The team had scored 16 points in 42 seconds to turn "The Game" into the "The Tie."

On Monday morning the headlines in The *Harvard Crimson* and The *Yale Daily News* were identical: "HARVARD WINS 29–29!" ★

JESSE'S JUMP

OLYMPIC ATHLETE JESSE OWENS OF THE
United States was accustomed to pressure. He always did well when he
was challenged on the track by other athletes. In one track championship competition in May, 1935, Jesse broke three world records and tied a
fourth. He was really looking forward to the 1936 Olympics.

Those Olympic Games presented a new kind of pressure to Jesse and the
other black athletes on the American team. The Games were being held in
Germany, where Adolf Hitler was the ruler. Since Hitler and his Nazi Party
preached that blacks weren't as good as whites, they believed the Olympics
would prove how much better white athletes were than black athletes. The
Nazis made the black athletes at the Games feel particularly uncomfortable.
Luckily the German fans didn't seem to share their leader's feelings and they
cheered loudly for all of the Olympic competitors—black and white.

On the first day of the competition, Hitler showed his prejudice. The first
gold medal of the Games was won by Hans Woellke of Germany. Woellke was
led to Hitler's box where he personally congratulated the winner. The second
gold medal went to Finnish athlete Ilmari Salminen; Hitler also offered him a
personal handshake. Then Cornelius Johnson, a black high jumper from California, won the third goal medal. All eyes turned to Hitler's box, but the Nazi
leader wasn't there anymore. As the public address announcer explained, the
German Chancellor had left the stadium because it was very late in the day
and a light rain was falling.

*J*ohnson wasn't really surprised that Hitler snubbed him. He winked at Jesse Owens, who was favored to win at least three gold medals during the Games. "Wait 'til you see what he does when you win," Johnson told Jesse.

"I didn't come over to shake hands with Hitler anyway," Jesse replied.

Jesse never did get to see what Hitler's reaction would be. The German leader did not return to the stadium during the remainder of the Games. Told by the International Olympic Committee that he must congratulate all the athletes or none at all, Hitler chose the second option.

Jesse did win his first gold medal the next day. Getting off to a fast start in the 100-meter finals, he held off all challengers to win the race by a full meter.

But the pressure seemed to get to Jesse on the next day. He was trying to qualify for the finals in the long jump. That was Jesse's best event, and he already held the world record. He leaped 26' 8½" during a track meet in 1935. That jump would not be beaten for almost 25 years.

On this day, however, Jesse was having trouble leaping the 23' 5½" needed to qualify for the long jump finals. Each competitor had three jumps to make the qualifying distance. When Jesse first went over to the jumping area, he saw several other athletes practicing. Jesse took an easy practice jump while he was still wearing his sweatshirt. To his shock, the officials counted that as his first qualifying jump. Because he hadn't really been trying, Jesse's jump was far short of the qualifying distance. Now he had only two more chances.

As he prepared for his second jump, Jesse was a little upset. He went far enough this time, but he stepped over the starting board before he left the ground. That was a foul, and the jump didn't count. Jesse had to qualify on the third jump. If he failed, he would be out of the competition. Now the pressure was really on, and he was feeling it. Trying to get his thoughts together, he paced along the sidelines.

Just then, a tall, blond man walked up to Jesse. He was Luz Long, the best German long jumper. Long stuck out his hand and said in broken English, "I'm Luz Long. I don't think we've met."

"Glad to meet you," Jesse said. "How are you?"

"I'm fine," Long said, "but how are *you*? You should be able to qualify with your eyes closed. Why don't you draw a line a few inches in back of the board and start your takeoff from there?"

It took a lot of guts for Luz Long to talk to Jesse Owens, a black man, in

front of thousands of people, including many Nazi leaders. But the German wasn't worried about what other people thought of him. He was talking to a fellow athlete, and he didn't care if that athlete was white or black.

Jesse followed the advice. He drew a line a full foot in front of the starting board and left the ground at that spot on his third jump. He qualified for the finals with almost a foot to spare.

In the long jump finals Jesse Owens and Luz Long put on a great battle. First Jesse set an Olympic record with a jump of 25' 10". Then Luz matched that distance exactly. Responding to the challenge, Jesse leaped more than 26 feet on his next jump to set a *new* Olympic record. Luz couldn't match that one. He knew he would have to settle for the silver medal. Jesse had one more jump, and he went all out once again.

He proved he was the best long jumper in the world with still *another* Olympic record leap of 26' 5½".

Who was the first person to shake Jesse's hand after his great jump? You guessed it—Luz Long!

The two long jumpers talked several more times during the Games. Luz watched his new friend earn two more gold medals—in the 200-meter dash and the 400-meter relay race. In many ways Jesse owed his success during the 1936 Olympics to the confidence-building talk the two men had had before that last qualifying jump.

Jesse and Luz never saw each other again. Soon after the 1936 Olympics, Luz joined the German army. He was killed during a battle in World War II. After the war Jesse came to Germany and met Luz's widow and son. He told them how sorry he was about his friend's death. He also described that day in Berlin and explained how important Luz's words had been to him. "It took a lot of courage for him to befriend me in front of Hitler," Jesse said.

Later Jesse wrote, "You can melt down all the medals and cups I have, and they wouldn't be a plating on the 24-carat friendship I felt for Luz Long at that moment when we talked."

Although the 1936 Olympic Games showed politics and athletics mixing in the worst possible way, the Games also showed that the spirit of friendly athletic competition could win out over prejudice and hatred. Jesse Owens gave four gold medal performances during the 1936 Olympics, but Luz Long's courage was just as golden. ★

A WILD GARDEN PARTY

HERE'S A RIDDLE: WHAT HAD THREE OVERTIMES, two game-saving last-second shots, one illegal time-out call, one near fight between a referee and several fans, one coach who collapsed from tension and more drama than almost any other basketball game in history? The answer is the fifth game of the 1976 National Basketball Association (NBA) finals.

Boston Garden has been the site of hundreds of NBA playoff games. After all, the Boston Celtics have won the league championship 16 times—more than any other team. However, no playoff game at the Garden was quite as wild as the one held there on June 4, 1976.

The Celtics were playing the Phoenix Suns in the finals. Rated the top team in the NBA's Eastern Conference that year, Boston was a heavy favorite to beat the Suns. Lucky just to be in the finals, the Phoenix Suns had finished the regular season with only the third best record in the Western Conference. They had to upset both the Seattle Supersonics and the Golden State Warriors to earn the right to play Boston for the championship.

he Celtics were led by such veteran stars as John Havlicek, Dave Cowens, Jo Jo White and Paul Silas. Those players had also helped Boston win the NBA title two years earlier. Before the 1975–76 season began, the Celtics had added a great shooter named Charley Scott to the team. They had acquired Scott in a trade with Phoenix.

On the other hand, the Suns were mostly young and inexperienced. Two of the team's top players were rookies—center Alvan Adams and guard Ricky Sobers. The only player with any playoff experience was Paul Westphal, who had played for the Celtics. He had come to Phoenix in the trade with Boston for Charley Scott.

At first the experts who had picked Boston to win seemed to be right. The Celtics easily won the first two games of the final round. Those games were played in Boston Garden, and the Celtics seldom lost there—particularly in the playoffs. Then the two teams headed out west for the next two games. If Boston won those, the series would be over. They would sweep the Suns four games to none.

But Phoenix wasn't about to be swept away. Playing at home, the Suns regained their winning touch. They scored a solid 105–98 victory in Game 3. Two nights later, Phoenix evened up the series with a tight

109–107 win. Some Boston fans wondered what was going on. They had not really expected such tough play from the Suns.

Absolutely no one expected what happened in Game 5 in Boston Garden!

The Celtics were obviously glad to be back on their home court. Jo Jo White made almost every shot he took in the first quarter, and Dave Cowens grabbed almost every rebound. When the horn sounded to end the period, Boston was ahead 36–18. It looked like the game was going to be a blowout.

The Celts added to their lead in the second period. At one time Boston was ahead by 22 points. Phoenix made a small dent in the lead, but the Suns still trailed by 16 at the half, 61–45.

After the halftime break some strange things began to happen. Suddenly Phoenix couldn't miss a shot, and Boston couldn't make any! The Suns outscored the Celtics 23–7 during the first part of the third period, including 11 straight points to tie the game at 68–68.

In the fourth quarter Boston rebuilt its lead. The Celtics were ahead by 7 points, then 9, then 11. With the Celtics ahead 94–83 and with just a few minutes left in the game, Boston fans began to relax. They were sure their team was headed for yet another league championship. Only

The Boston Celtics and their fans celebrate another clutch basket by forward John Havlicek in the 1976 NBA championship series against Phoenix.

one more game after this one, and then . . . .

Then the Suns began another dramatic rally, and Boston's 11-point lead quickly began to crumble. Suddenly it was all gone. Phoenix had scored 11 straight points in the closing minutes of a playoff game against the Celtics—in Boston Garden! That was almost unthinkable! With only 39 seconds to go, the game was tied once again, 94–94.

The Suns had their first chance to win the game. When forward Curtis Perry went to the foul line, he made one free throw. It was now 95–94, Phoenix.

With less than 10 seconds to play, John Havlicek was fouled. If he made both free throws, the Celts would probably win. He made only one, though; that meant the score was 95–95. Havlicek got the ball back with only three seconds left. He sent a game-winning shot toward the basket, but it bounced off the rim. The game went into overtime.

That first overtime was intense. Neither team could get anything going on offense. With only seconds remaining, Phoenix was up by two points. Then Havlicek sank a clutch basket to tie it up once more. That was game-saving basket number 1.

During the second overtime period everything went crazy. Phoenix was clinging to a one-point lead with only a few seconds remaining. Havli-

cek, who had the ball, began racing along the left side of the court. He flung a running one-hand shot toward the basket, and it banked in. Boston now led by one—and there was only one second left.

Excited Boston fans stormed onto the court to congratulate their heroes. But the game wasn't over! Referee Richie Powers held two fingers over his head to signal that there were still two seconds remaining in the game. Because they were ready for the game to end, some fans attacked Powers. Police rushed onto the court, rescued Powers and arrested his attackers. Meanwhile Boston coach Tom Heinsohn, who was suffering from stomach problems, nearly collapsed from all of the tension. Forced to rest, he stood by helplessly as his assistant gave directions to the team.

Now Phoenix had a big problem. The Suns had to go the full length of the court and score in only two seconds. That seemed impossible, especially with the tension in the Garden. Normally the Suns could call a timeout. In that case, they would get the ball at mid-court to start their final play. But Phoenix didn't have any timeouts left. What could they do?

Paul Westphal, the former Celtic, had a plan. What if the team called a timeout anyway? The penalty for calling an illegal timeout would be one penalty foul shot for Boston. Phoenix would then get the ball at mid-court. If the Suns could make a basket, the game would be tied, and they would go into a third overtime period.

Phoenix coach John MacLeod followed Westphal's advice and called the timeout. Jo Jo White sank the penalty shot to put Boston up by 2 points. The clock still read 0:01. Curtis Perry threw a pass to Suns forward Garfield Heard. Heard turned quickly toward the basket and sent up a high arcing shot. It looked like a rainbow. While the shot was still in the air, the buzzer sounded. In a flash, the ball swished through the hoop. That was game-saving basket Number 2. The score was tied—again!

No one could believe it. Boston fans were still surrounding the court. They had been waiting to charge back out again to celebrate the big win. However, the only ones celebrating now were the Suns players! No championship game had ever gone into a third overtime before. The fans were watching basketball history being made.

The Celtics decided to put the game away for good in the third overtime. They broke out to a 6-point lead with 36 seconds to go. Ricky Sobers of Phoenix made a basket,

Boston's Jim Ard sank two foul shots, and Paul Westphal followed with another Suns score. Boston's lead was now 4 points with less than 15 seconds remaining. No sweat, right? Wrong! Westphal stole the ball and made a layup to pull Phoenix within two points. There were still 12 seconds to go. Would that be enough time for another miracle? No. Boston's Jo Jo White dribbled out the remaining seconds to save the Celtics win.

Although the Boston players congratulated each other, they were much too tired to celebrate. Instead, they gave a sigh of relief and helped each other off the court. It had been the longest night in NBA championship history, and the series wasn't even over yet!

Two nights later Boston closed out the Suns with a seven-point win in Phoenix. That game was pretty tame in comparison—no fights between fans and referees, no over-exhausted coaches and no last-second baskets. In a strange way, both teams were probably a little relieved when Boston won Game 6. If the Suns had won, they would have headed back to Boston for a seventh game with the Celtics. Neither team was ready for another wild Boston Garden party! ★

SOLO SUPERSTARS

Joe Montana of the San Francisco 49ers lofts another pass toward the end zone.

Sometimes even in a crowd or on a team, an athlete is all alone. Success depends on the athlete's talent, training, courage and calmness under pressure. At those nail-biting moments, it's important to have the right person on your team. Or better still, to be that one-in-a-million athlete who can accomplish what no one else can. Read on and discover the triumph of some of the greatest individual efforts in sports. Maybe they will inspire you to superhuman feats of your own! ★

Mary Lou Retton during her floor routine at the 1984 Summer Olympic Games in Los Angeles. She earned a "10"—a perfect score.

A DOUBLE PERFECT DAY

GYMNAST MARY LOU RETTON OF THE UNITED States knew that for the next few minutes, she had to be absolutely perfect. There could be no wrong steps, no slight slips, no unsteady landings. Mary Lou was going for a gold medal in the women's all-around championship in gymnastics at the 1984 Olympic Games. Her performance on the next two pieces of equipment would determine whether she was recognized as the best gymnast in the world—or only the second best.

The pressure was intense. Mary Lou was in a terrific battle with Ecaterina (Kati) Szabo of Romania for the title. Each young woman had to perform in four different gymnastic events: the balance beam, the uneven bars, the side horse vault and the floor exercise. Their scores for the four events would be added together. Whoever had the highest total would be awarded the gold medal as the all-around champion.

Kati and Mary Lou would be taking part in different events at the same time. For example, while Kati was performing on the balance beam in one part of the arena, Mary Lou would be on the uneven bars in another location.

After the first two events, the scores stood: Szabo 59.325, Retton 59.175. Mary Lou had to make up .15 points in only two events. Since Kati would probably record near perfect scores in her final two events, Mary Lou knew she would have to be even better than *near* perfect. Luckily, Mary Lou's final two events would be the floor exercise and vault—her two best. But it was going to take a flawless performance in each event to get the gold.

While other gymnasts relied on graceful movements in the various events, Mary Lou's performances involved power and great strength. Most gymnasts did a flip and twisted their bodies one full turn while airborne in the vault event. Instead Mary Lou did both a flip and a double twist. She also did double back somersaults in the air during her floor exercise program. It took amazing strength to stay in control of her body during these daring movements. And Mary Lou was very strong.

She was also quite mature for a 16-year-old. Part of that maturity was the result of Mary Lou's having left home when she was 14. She had moved from West Virginia, where she grew up, to Texas to work with Bela Karolyi, one of the world's outstanding gymnastics coaches.

Karolyi had first noticed Mary Lou at a meet in Salt Lake City, Utah. At that time, she was 13 and was not ranked as one of the top young gymnasts in America. Karolyi saw that Mary Lou had a lot of natural ability, but not enough training. When he invited her to work with him in Houston, her parents refused at first. How could they let their youngest child leave the family? A year later Mary Lou's parents finally gave in.

What followed were two years of unbelievably hard work. Karolyi had helped to make Romania one of the world's great gymnastics powers; he had trained such world champions as Nadia Comaneci, who was the 1976 Olympic all-around gold medalist. In 1981, Karolyi had decided to leave Romania and come to the United States. He felt he needed more freedom in his life and in his teaching.

Karolyi wanted his students to be strong mentally and physically. He started Mary Lou on a tough running and exercise program. After this preliminary training he began working with her in the various gymnastics events. He pushed and pushed. When Mary Lou felt as though she would collapse or fail, Karolyi would yell, "You can do it! You can do it!" When she did accomplish a difficult task, he would reward her with a big, warm bear hug.

When she was 15, Mary Lou entered her first big meet, the

McDonald's America Cup, which was held in New York's Madison Square Garden. Mary Lou surprised everyone but Karolyi and herself with her performance in New York. At the end of the two-day competition, Mary Lou had recorded six scores of 9.9 (10 is a perfect score). Suddenly she had risen from an unknown to the Number 1 female gymnast in America.

Immediately she began working toward the 1984 Olympics Games, which were going to be held in Los Angeles. Mary Lou had a special mission. No woman from the U.S. had ever won any medal at all in Olympic gymnastic history. She planned to rewrite that bit of history. And she wanted to do it in America.

Mary Lou knew that her main competitor in Los Angeles was going to be Ecaterina Szabo. Considered the outstanding junior gymnast in Europe in 1980 and 1982, Szabo had gotten five perfect 10s in the world championships in 1983.

Mary Lou told reporters, "I've seen her work. She's terrific! But there's one thing she doesn't know about me. I'm tougher than she is."

Soon Mary Lou would prove her toughness to everyone. Six weeks before the Olympics, tragedy struck. One morning Mary Lou woke up and couldn't bend her knee. Tears of pain and frustration filled her eyes. Would she have to give up her Olympic dream?

Mary Lou was flown to Richmond, Virginia, where a team of doctors performed arthroscopic surgery on her knee. This type of operation involves inserting a special scope into the knee and removing any pieces of loose bone or cartilage. The doctors found three small pieces of cartilage behind her knee cap. When these were taken out, Mary Lou could bend her knee without pain. It can take months to recover from a regular knee operation; it usually takes several weeks to recover from arthroscopic surgery. Mary Lou had just six weeks until the Olympics began. Everyone doubted that she would be ready in time.

The day after her surgery, though, Mary Lou was back in the gym in Houston. She amazed everyone by climbing aboard an exercise bike and putting her knee to the test. Within two weeks she was handling flips and landings as well as before she had hurt her knee.

Now, it was August 3, 1984. Mary Lou's performances in the first two events of the all-around had assured her of becoming America's first women's all-around gymnastics medalist. But she wanted more; she wanted the gold. It was going to take perfection to gain it.

Spectators gasped as she opened her floor exercise program with a high-flying double back somersault.

One reporter said Mary Lou's body looked like a knife thrown into the air as she spun above the ground. Before the routine was over, she completed three more double back somersaults and landed perfectly each time. The crowd began roaring for a perfect score, and the judges agreed. When she saw the big "10" on the scoreboard, Mary Lou jumped excitedly.

Nearby, Szabo completed her vault performance. Her landing was just a tiny bit shaky, and her score reflected that small error. It was a 9.90. With one event to go, Mary Lou was just .05 behind her Romanian opponent.

As Mary Lou prepared for her vault, the crowd turned its attention to Kati on the uneven bars. She was beautiful. Only a few slight imperfections kept her from recording a 10 and locking up the gold medal. Mary Lou watched Kati too. "It was a nice set, a clean set," she said. "But she took a step on her dismount, and I knew it would be a 9.9. I knew I had it."

While the judges debated Kati's score, Mary Lou got set for her first of two vaults. She took a last look at Karolyi on the sidelines. Then she punched the air with her fist and began racing the 80 feet to the side horse. The secret to the vault is speed on the runway. Mary Lou ran faster than she ever had before. She bounced on the small springboard in front of the horse. After lightly touching the horse, she propelled herself high into the air and did a complete flip and a double twist. She landed flat on her feet, without even a slight wobble. She knew it had been perfect.

A few seconds later everyone else knew too. Mary Lou and Kati's scores were flashed to the crowd: Retton 10.0, Szabo 9.9. Mary Lou had her gold medal. She had won it under extreme pressure, in front of the home crowd.

"Who could do it? Who could come back and do it?" Karolyi said aftwards. "I gurantee no gymnast in the world could have done what Mary Lou has."

For Mary Lou Retton, August 3, 1984, was a perfect day. It was double perfect. ★

ENOS SLAUGHTER'S MAD DASH

HERE WERE TWO OUTS IN THE BOTTOM OF THE eighth inning in the seventh game of the 1946 World Series. The St. Louis Cardinals and Boston Red Sox were tied three games apiece and 3–3 in the seventh and final game. The Cardinals were at bat and needed one run to take the lead.

Perched on first base, representing that go-ahead run, was Cardinals outfielder Enos Slaughter. He was the perfect man for the job. Nobody in baseball outhustled Enos Slaughter. If anyone could find a way to score, it was Enos.

Enos Slaughter ran everywhere. He ran onto and off of the baseball field at the beginning and end of each inning. He ran to first base when he drew a walk. He usually would make it from first base to third base on his teammates' hits. Even when he knew he was going to be out on a ground ball or a pop fly, he ran as hard as he could. In the field he would chase down every ball hit near him. He would even run head-first into a wall in order to catch a fly ball. That may sound a little reckless to you, but that's the way Enos Slaughter liked to play baseball.

nos began running when he was a teenager playing in the minor leagues. At the end of one inning, he began trotting in from the outfield to the bench. Then he slowed to a walk. His manager yelled, "Hey kid, if you're tired, I'll get you some help!" Embarrassed by his coach's remark, Enos never slowed down after that.

Enos joined the St. Louis Cardinals in 1938. Of course he *quickly* became a star. In only his second year in the majors, he hit .320. He would end up hitting .300 or better in 10 different seasons during his career.

Enos's running may have knocked him out of a chance to play in the 1941 World Series—literally. One day in August, he and a teammate were both chasing a fly ball. To avoid a collision, Enos jumped over the teammate and landed shoulder-first onto the concrete wall in the outfield. Knocked out cold for a few seconds, he had to be helped off the field. He had a broken collarbone and was out for the next five weeks. Without Enos in the lineup, the Cardinals fell behind the Brooklyn Dodgers in the 1941 pennant race. They finished the season 2 1/2 games behind.

Enos got another chance in 1942, and made the most of it. He led the National League in total hits that year and was also Number One in triples. You have to run hard to make a triple; it wasn't surprising that Enos

was the NL's triples king. Enos's Cardinals not only ran away with the pennant, they also raced by the New York Yankees in the World Series.

In 1943 Enos was ready to begin another great season when he was drafted into the Army Air Force. He spent the next three years of World War II at various air bases in the Pacific.

In 1946 Enos was back. The Cardinals and Dodgers were neck-and-neck throughout the season. At the end of the year, they were in a dead heat. For the first time in league history there was going to be a best two-out-of-three-game playoff series to decide the pennant winner. Enos hit two singles in the first game, a 4–2

9th inning to tie the game and once in the 10th to win it.

St. Louis won Game 2, but Boston took the series lead back with a 4–0 win in Game 3. In Game 4 Enos went to work. He hit a home run, a double and two singles to lead St. Louis to a 12–3 victory. That win evened the series at 2–2.

The Red Sox won Game 5. In doing so, they almost knocked Enos Slaughter out of the series for good. In the fourth inning of the game Enos was hit with a pitch on his elbow. True to form, he picked himself up and raced down to first base, even though he was in terrible pain. A few pitches later he stole second base.

After the game, doctors examined Enos's elbow and discovered a blood clot. One doctor said, "Don't play any more this year. You might hurt the arm more and never be able to play again."

Enos wouldn't listen to the doctors. He begged his manager to put him in the lineup in Game 6. Finally the manager gave in. Even though he could barely hold a bat, Enos was able to hit a single in the third inning to drive in a run. The Cardinals won the game 4–1 to send the series into a seventh game.

So far the World Series had followed a pattern. The Red Sox had won Games 1, 3 and 5. The Cardinals had won Games 2, 4 and 6. If the trend held, Boston was going to win

St. Louis victory. Then he cracked a two-run triple for another Cardinals win in the second game. The Cardinals swept the playoff, and once again Enos Slaughter was in the World Series.

Enos hit a triple in the first game of the World Series against the Boston Red Sox. However, the hit was wasted, as Boston scored once in the its first World Series since the days when Babe Ruth pitched for the Sox in 1918. Enos and his teammates didn't want that to happen.

In that seventh game St. Louis opened up a 3–1 lead. In the top of the eighth inning the Red Sox scored twice off Cardinals pitcher Murry Dickson. The game was tied.

Enos led off the bottom of the eighth for St. Louis. Although his elbow was still hurting him, he hit a sharp single and raced to first base. Enos began thinking about how he could score the go-ahead run; he took a lead off first base. The next Cardinals hitter tried a bunt to move Enos to second base, but he popped up instead for the first out. The next hitter sent a short fly ball to the outfield. That made two outs, and Enos remained on first base. Up came Harry Walker, one of the Cardinals best hitters.

Walker slapped the ball over the Red Sox shortstop's head. It looked like a simple single. With Enos's speed that would put runners at first and third. However, as Enos went around second base, he took one quick look at where the Red Sox outfielders were located. He made up his mind right then to try to go all the way home. Enos seemed to shift into high gear at that moment. His third base coach had his hands up in the air. "Stop!" the coach shouted. But Enos wasn't about to stop.

By now Boston centerfielder Leon Culberson had picked up the ball in the outfield. He threw it to shortstop Johnny Pesky, who had gone out to take the relay. Pesky had his back to home plate, and no one had told him that Enos Slaughter was trying to score on the play. Thinking he could throw out Walker, the Sox shortstop turned to his right and looked toward second base.

Suddenly Pesky saw what was really happening. He set himself for a throw home, but he was slightly off balance. Enos easily slid across home plate before the weak throw got there. The score was now 4–3, St. Louis. That was how the game ended, as Boston failed to score in the ninth inning. The Cardinals won the World Series because Enos Slaughter kept running and never slowed down.

Enos's mad dash around the bases helped earn him a place in Baseball's Hall of Fame. He probably ran all the way from his home in North Carolina to Cooperstown, New York, where the Baseball Hall of Fame is located, to receive that honor! ★

SPINNING HIS WHEELS

GREG LEMOND SPENT THE SUMMER OF 1989 riding his bicycle through France. As he rode all over the country— over hills and mountains, through valleys, into and out of hundreds of towns and cities, he never looked at the beautiful countryside or the charming villages he passed. Instead, people looked at him. More than 10 million people watched him pump, pedal and push himself to go faster. Throughout the ride, a clock was ticking. Every second counted—*every* second. Greg LeMond was trying to become the second American in 86 years to win the most famous bicycle race in the world— the Tour de France. Who was the first American to do it? Greg LeMond, three years earlier.

The Tour de France is one of the greatest challenges in sports. For 23 days the world's finest cyclists race against the clock and each other. The Tour is divided into several sections, called stages. One stage may be a climb through the Pyrenees mountains, which separate France from Spain. Another stage may be a spin around the tiny country of Luxembourg. Other stages may take riders on roads that wind through fields of sunflowers or world-famous vineyards. The race course varies every year, but it is usually well over 2,000 miles in total length. The final stage in 1989 was a time trial, or sprint, from Versailles to Paris—a distance of 27 kilometers (a little over 16 miles).

In a time trial, racers don't ride next to each other as they do in a regular race. Instead they start out separately, two minutes apart. While judges record each rider's time on stopwatches, riders compete against the clock and have to wait to see how their times compare with their opponents' times. The final time trial in the 1989 Tour de France was going to be something special.

In the first 22 days of the 1989 race, Greg LeMond traveled more than 2,000 miles in a little over 87 hours. As the 23rd day began he found himself 50 seconds behind the leader, Laurent Fignon of France. It might just as well have been 50 hours! Greg had only 27 kilometers to make up the time difference. His former coach, Paul Koechli, said, "It's possible for Greg to grab a second a kilometer, but two? Unthinkable!"

Greg was more hopeful. He knew it was going to be difficult but he thought it was still possible.

No one could tell Greg it was "unthinkable." After all, it was a miracle that he was even in the race. After he won the Tour de France in 1986 Greg went through some terrible times and was lucky to be alive. In April 1987, nine months after his big win, Greg was hunting wild turkeys with his brother-in-law. Greg was wearing camouflage clothing and hiding in some bushes. His brother-in-law saw a sudden movement in the bushes and fired his shotgun. The blast sent 60 steel pellets into Greg's chest and lower body.

As he lay bleeding on the ground, Greg moaned, "I'm never going to ride again." But he did. Doctors were amazed at how quickly Greg recovered after the operation. They credited his recovery to his excellent physical condition and to his strong will to get better. Greg still has 40 shotgun pellets inside his body (several in the lining of his heart), but they haven't stopped him from competing.

Once he got out of the hospital Greg began training again. However, a few months later he had a sudden attack of appendicitis, an illness in which your appendix, an organ inside your body, gets irritated and makes you *very* sick. This meant that doctors had to perform another emergency operation to remove his appendix in order to save his life.

Greg went back into training a few months after that. Then he noticed a problem with his right leg; it easily grew tired and became painful. Doctors took X-rays and discovered that several tendons had been injured. That meant another operation for Greg. When he learned that he had anemia (not enough iron in his blood), he had to take medicine to correct that condition. All these difficulties would have stopped most people, but not Greg LeMond. He was determined to get back onto the professional cycling tour in Europe. And he was determined to win his second Tour de France.

Slowly Greg worked himself back into shape. It wasn't easy. Not only did he have to build up his strength, but also he had to rebuild his confidence. Most cycling experts thought

Greg's career was over.

One big test in 1989 was an Italian race called the Giro d'Italia, which took place a month before the Tour de France. Most of the top racers entered. Laurent Fignon won the Giro. Greg came in 39th in the race—nearly an hour behind the leader. That finish didn't exactly build Greg's confidence, but it didn't stop him, either.

For most of the first 20 stages of the 1989 Tour de France, the lead passed back and forth between Fignon and LeMond. After each stage, the leader was permitted to wear a special yellow jersey throughout the next stage. Greg first earned the right to wear the leader's jersey when he won a time trial in the fifth stage of race. Sprinting was Greg's strong suit. He had more trouble with the long, demanding climbs along mountain roads.

Greg kept the yellow jersey for five days. Fignon overtook him during a climbing stage. Fignon began to brag. "I showed [LeMond] I was the strongest," Fignon said. "If he wants the yellow jersey, he'll have to walk over my body."

Fignon wore the yellow jersey for the next five days as the riders began heading north again toward the finish line in Paris. However, Greg was slowly making up the time difference that separated him from Fignon. The 15th stage was a 39-kilometer (about

24 miles) uphill time trial. As the riders began the stage, Fignon held a 7-second lead, but Greg outdid him by 47 seconds. He won the yellow jersey back and had a 40-second advantage over Fignon.

The riders headed into the French Alps for the next several stages. On the steep climbs, Fignon regained the lead and then stretched it. Going into the 21st and final stage, the Frenchman was up by a "gigantic" 50 seconds.

For that final 27-kilometer (about 17 miles) time trial, the riders started in reverse order of their total time. That meant Greg would be next-to-last and Fignon last. Since the two riders would start out 2 minutes apart, Greg had to hope that Fignon would finish at least 2 minutes and 50 seconds after he did.

"It's possible," Greg said. "It's still possible."

During the entire 27 kilometers he never let up. Halfway through the final stage, he had closed the gap to 21 seconds. Unbelievably Greg was making up nearly two seconds a kilometer! As he entered the final part of the race along the most famous street in Paris, the Champs Elysées, Greg was almost flying. The hundreds of thousands of people crowding the street began cheering him on. *"Vive LeMond!* [Long live LeMond!]" they shouted. *"Vive LeMond!"*

Greg cut every turn on the race course sharply. He needed to save every second he could. He nearly caught up with Pedro Delgado, who had started two minutes before him. As he crossed the finish line, Greg heard his time: 26 minutes and 57 seconds. He had averaged nearly 34 miles per hour for the final stage! That was some pace! Would it be good enough?

Now Fignon was racing along the Champs Elysées as his French countrymen cheered even louder than they had for LeMond. Fignon's legs pumped at top speed as the clock reached 27 minutes. Then 27 minutes and 30 seconds . . . 40 seconds . . . 45 seconds . . . . Fignon crossed the finish line at 27 minutes and 55 seconds. Greg LeMond had won the Tour de France by eight seconds! That was the closest margin in the race's 86-year history.

The television cameras captured two very different scenes near the finish line. In one scene Greg LeMond and his wife Kathy were hugging and cheering. In the other, Laurent Fignon lay exhausted on the ground while his coaches and friends comforted him. What a difference those few seconds made!

In French the name LeMond means "the world." At that moment in August 1989, Greg LeMond was on top of the world. *"Vive LeMond!"* ★

ONE GOOD LEG, TWO GOOD ARMS

*T*HE LOS ANGELES DODGERS NEEDED SOMEONE to save them. The Oakland Athletics were leading the Dodgers, 4–3, in the bottom of the ninth inning of the first game of the 1988 World Series. A Dodgers runner was on first base with the tying run, but who could knock him in? Dodgers fans wanted Kirk Gibson; they needed Kirk Gibson. But Gibson's knee hurt so badly that he could barely walk. How could he possibly hit?

Kirk Gibson had been saving the Los Angeles Dodgers all year. Although he hadn't led the National League in batting in 1988, his hits seemed to have come at the most important moments. His 25 home runs had not led the league either, but many had won games for the Dodgers. Cartoonists in Los Angeles sometimes pictured "Gibby" with a big "S" on the front of his uniform. That stood for "Superman." He was that important to the team.

Then in the National League playoff series against the New York Mets, Kirk showed that he was truly the Dodgers leader. The Mets were favored to win and they took two of the first three playoff games against the Dodgers. When Gibson came to bat in the 12th inning of Game 4 he smacked a home run to win it. That evened up the series. Kirk continued his heroics in Game 5. Early in the game he walloped another home run way over the fence in New York's Shea Stadium. That blast drove in three runs to put L.A. ahead. When the Mets closed in again, Gibby went back to work. He got an infield hit in the ninth inning, then stole second base to set up an important run.

On the steal he pulled a muscle in his leg; this same muscle had been a problem for him all year. Kirk had to be helped from the field. As he left, Mets fans gave him a loud ovation. The cheering was a mixture of respect and relief. The fans were happy that Kirk couldn't hurt the Mets any more that day.

No one figured Kirk would be able to play during the rest of the series. However, he was back in Game 6. Gibby didn't do much in the last two games of the playoff series. What he did do was to injure his knee while sliding into second base in the seventh game. Still, his courage alone helped to inspire his teammates. They edged out the Mets in the seventh game to earn a spot in the World Series.

This time the Dodgers opponents would be the Oakland A's, the team with the best record that year. Boasting a lot of power in Jose Canseco and Mark McGwire, Oakland also had the best pitching in baseball. The A's starting pitcher Dave Stewart was a 20-game winner for the second year in a row, and ace relief pitcher Dennis Eckersley was almost unhittable.

The Dodgers were missing their most important player, Kirk Gibson. Doctors said that he might not be able to play at all during the Series. In the first game Canseco got the A's off

It wasn't pretty, but he got the job done—an ailing Kirk Gibson manages to connect for a game-winning home run off Oakland's ace reliever, Dennis Eckersley.

to a big lead with a grand slam home run, which scored four runs. L.A. came back slowly, and the score was 4–3 as the Dodgers came to bat in the bottom of the ninth.

Eckersley was on the mound for Oakland. He had a strange sidearm delivery that scared most right-handed batters. They thought the ball was going to hit them, and they would back away from the plate as the pitch came. Then the ball would just zip by for a strike, or the batter would hit it weakly for an easy out. Eckersley was pretty tough on left-handers too. Dodgers fans wondered if their favorite left-hander, Kirk Gibson, would get a chance to bat against "The Eck."

The A's reliever got the first two Dodgers out in the ninth to move Oakland to within one *out* of a victory. Then pinch hitter Mike Davis drew a walk. That was pretty amazing; Eckersley seldom walked a batter. Two outs, one on. It was time for a hero to save the day. Dodgers manager Tommy Lasorda looked down his bench. Kirk Gibson nodded.

As Gibby limped over to the bat rack and then toward home plate, Dodger fans stood and cheered wildly. But they were also a little worried because Kirk could barely walk. He would need to put weight onto his bad knee in order to hit the ball.

Gibby swung weakly at the first pitch and fouled it off. It was clear that the knee was hurting him. He gritted his teeth and fouled off a second pitch. It looked like Eckersely was going to win this battle. There was nothing wrong with Kirk's eyes, however. He let three close ones go by to force the full count, three balls and two strikes.

The next pitch was right in Kirk's "power alley." By pushing the bat on the ball, he put as little weight on his right knee as possible. The ball zoomed off the bat; it headed straight for the rightfield stands. It was a home run! The Dodgers had won!

Kirk didn't run around the bases. He did a combination of a skip and a hop—mostly using his left leg. He pumped his fist in the air and kept shouting. Kirk Gibson had saved the Dodgers once again. For Dodgers fans, he was a real live Superman.

The whole job wasn't done. Los Angeles had to win three more games to take the series. They handled that task easily, taking three of the next four games. The A's just couldn't rebound from the shock of Gibson's home run. For the Dodgers that home run gave them the confidence they needed to go on and become world champions. Kirk Gibson had two strong arms and only one strong leg on October 15, 1989, but he helped carry an entire team to victory. ★

A New Queen in England

WOULD ANY WOMAN BEAT MARTINA NAVRATILOVA at Wimbledon? That question was on every tennis fan's mind as the 111-year-old British tournament opened in June 1988. No one had been able to beat her between 1982 and 1987. For six straight years "Queen Martina" ruled over Wimbledon where she had played 47 singles matches on the grass courts and had won them all.

During most of those years Martina had been ranked Number 1 in the world in women's tennis. As the 1988 championship began at Wimbledon, Martina found herself in a strange position—one she didn't like very much. She was Number 2. A German teenager named Steffi Graf had replaced her at the top.

In 1987 the two women had played an amazing match for the Wimbledon title. That was Steffi's first time in the Wimbledon finals. Martina had much more experience, and she used it. Even though Steffi played brilliantly in the first set of that '87 match, Martina kept hitting the ball to her backhand side. Whenever Steffi made a weak hit or a mistake, Martina struck with a winning shot. Martina won the match in two close sets. However, if one or two points had gone the other way, Steffi might well have been the champ.

n 1988 Steffi was ready for Martina. That year the West German had already won the Australian and French Open tournaments without losing a single set. Those victories had helped her earn the Number 1 ranking. If she could also win at Wimbledon and the U.S. Open, she would capture the "Grand Slam," which means winning those four tournaments in the same year. Only two other women in tennis history had done that.

Martina had a few special reasons of her own for wanting to win the 1988 Wimbledon tournament. She was closing in on a 50-year-old tennis record. In the 1920s and 1930s, a woman named Helen Wills Moody of the United States had won eight Wimbledon titles and 50 straight matches. A win would give Martina her ninth Wimbledon crown and put her ahead of Moody; a win would also give her 48 straight matches without a loss. She planned to break the record of 50 straight in 1989.

Tennis fans in the stadium in England and those watching on television around the world got set for the fireworks. This was going to be a match of power against power. No woman could hit the ball harder than Martina or Steffi. Steffi was younger and a little quicker, but Martina was a veteran who almost always found a way to win.

Just as she had the year before, Martina began attacking Steffi's backhand in the first set. This time Steffi was better prepared. Having practiced for several weeks against a lefthanded friend because Martina was lefthanded, Steffi had made sure her friend had concentrated on hitting to her backhand.

With the score 2–2 in the first set, Martina was serving. Steffi needed one point to win on Martina's serve. Martina hit a rifle shot to Steffi's backhand, and the ball came back even harder. The backhand winner put Steffi in the driver's seat in the match. Or so people thought.

Steffi went up 5–3 and needed just one more game to take the first set. She never got it. Suddenly Martina raised the level of her game another notch. She rallied to win her serve twice and to break Steffi's serve two times as well. By the time Steffi realized what was happening, Martina was heading off the court with a 7–5 first set victory. It was the first set Steffi had lost in the matches thus far in the tournament.

Immediately taking control in the second set, just as she had in 1987, Martina jumped ahead 2–0 with a service win and a break. Then Martina made a tactical error. With the score tied at 15–15 (they had each won one point) in the third game, Martina decided to attack Steffi's powerful forehand. She figured she

would surprise her opponent, but Steffi wasn't fooled at all. She slammed the ball right past Martina to go up 15–30.

On the next point, Steffi had to use her great speed. Martina saw that Steffi was playing way back near the baseline at the end of the court. She decided to hit a soft shot, called a drop shot, just over the net. Graf raced in at full speed to get to the ball before it bounced twice, and got there in time to slap the ball past a surprised Navratilova. Now the score was 15–40. Steffi needed one more point to break Martina's serve and get back into the match. She won her point when Martina chose to test her forehand again. Steffi hit a rocket service return for a winner.

With those three shots the entire match turned around. Steffi took control and showed why she was ranked Number 1 in the world. She pounded shot after shot past her opponent. She won the next game to even the second set at 2–2. Then she won four more games in a row to win the set 6–2.

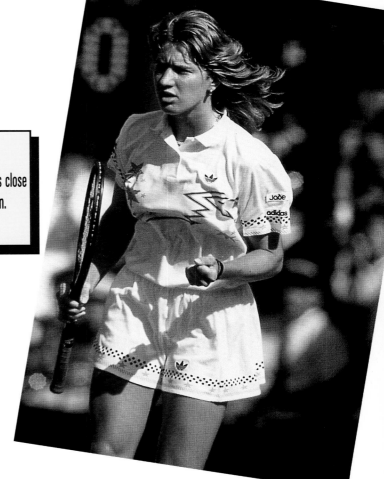

In the third set Martina had to face three different opponents. There was Steffi of course. There was also a steady drizzle that kept fogging up Martina's glasses. And then her back began to ache. Martina had been having trouble with her back throughout the year. Now was no time for it to flare up again, but it did.

Even if the skies had been clear and Martina's back had felt fine, there was no stopping Steffi Graf. The score went to 3–1, Graf. Then there was a 44-minute rain delay. During the wait, Martina had her back treated. Calm and confident, Steffi watched television. After the break Steffi closed out the match quickly with a 6–1 win in the third set.

Queen Martina had been forced to give up her throne, and a new queen had taken her place. The old queen stood by quietly as her successor was crowned. Then she slowly walked off the court.

Yes, someone had finally beaten Martina Navratilova at Wimbledon. But it had taken seven years to do it. ★

THE MAN WHO WOULDN'T SIT DOWN

PUT YOURSELF IN TED WILLIAMS' SHOES. You play outfield for the Boston Red Sox. You're the best all-around hitter in the American League. With one week to go in the season you're batting over .400. Nobody hits over .400! Since 1900, only seven men have ever broken that magic barrier. And you can join that special group.

You have worked hard all of the 1941 season, and you have done some great things. In early July you had the game-winning hit in the All-Star Game. You came to bat with two outs in the ninth and two men on base. The American League was behind 5–4. Then you sent a rocket more than 450 feet into the upper deck, and the American League wins it, 7–5.

Now it's September. With one week left in the season, you're leading the league in batting and home runs. And you're hitting .406. If you keep that average above .400, you will have a special spot in the baseball record books.

our manager has just come to you. He says, "Ted, we're out of the pennant race. The Sox aren't going to make the World Series this year, even if you get a hit every time up in the next week. But you've had such a great year. You're batting over four hundred. That's amazing. Why don't you sit out this week—as a reward? Don't risk that four hundred average by making a lot of outs this week. Just sit down."

What would you do?

Here is what Ted Williams did. He told his manager, Joe Cronin, "If I'm going to be a four hundred hitter, I want to earn it all the way."

Ted might have been sorry about his decision at first. In the next few days pitchers didn't give him any good pitches to hit. Facing Ted Williams was a battle for every pitcher in the American League. The pitchers wanted to win those battles. For the next few games they did. With one day remaining in the season Ted's average had dipped to .39955. Rounded off, that number was .400. Exactly .400. If Ted made one more

Ted Williams of the Boston Red Sox, the man said to have the sweetest swing in all of baseball.

out without getting a hit, the average would dip to .399. That's a terrific average, but it's not .400!

Once again Cronin came to his star. He said, "Ted, why don't you sit out the doubleheader tomorrow? No one will blame you for it. Why risk it?"

Ted's answer was the same as before. "Write me into your lineup, Skipper. I'm not sitting down."

It was cold and windy in Philadelphia that last day of the season. Neither the Philadelphia Athletics nor the Boston Red Sox were going to win the pennant. So the doubleheader they played was meaningless. That didn't keep the fans away, however. A large crowd came to watch Ted Williams try to become the first .400 hitter in the American League in 18 years.

Ted had gotten the nickname "The Splendid Splinter" because he was so skinny. He may not have been very heavy, but he had amazing strength. He had always been that way. At the age of 14, tenth-grader Ted Williams had walked up to the baseball coach at his high school in San Diego, California and asked for a tryout for the school team.

The coach looked at this skinny kid, then turned away. At the end of the practice the coach looked around. The skinny kid was still there. The coach decided to give him a chance. "O.K., kid, hit a few," the coach said.

Ted slapped pitch after pitch to all parts of the outfield. He hit a few long shots too. The coach knew he was watching a special player. "Kid, you want to play for Herbert Hoover High?" he asked.

During the next two seasons Ted led Herbert Hoover High to two San Diego County baseball championships. He hit .586 and .403 in those seasons. Then the pro scouts began coming around. The Yankees had a chance to sign Ted, but the team refused to give him the $1,000 bonus he asked for. Boy, would they regret that decision in later years!

Ted's mother didn't want him to leave home to play baseball, but Ted had an idea. San Diego had a top minor league team in the 1930s. Ted went to the manager of that team and asked for a tryout. The manager took one look at the skinny 17-year-old. He probably felt the same way that the high school coach had felt. Once again it took just a few minutes of batting practice to convince the coach to give Ted a chance.

Ted also wanted to be a pitcher in those days, but his pitching was terrible. So the manager found a place for Ted in the outfield. He wasn't too good a fielder either, but his bat made up for his poor fielding.

The Red Sox signed Ted after two seasons in San Diego. He spent one year playing for Boston's top minor league team in Minneapolis. There he hit .366 and led the league in batting in five different categories. In 1939 he arrived in Boston to stay.

Ted's first two seasons with the Red Sox were great, but his third was magnificent. At the end of that third season he was batting .400. And he refused to sit down.

As Ted came up for the first time in the doubleheader, most of the fans in the stands in Philadelphia were a little nervous. Not the Splendid Splinter. The umpire behind the plate gave Ted a bit of advice. "If you're going to hit four hundred, you've got to be loose," the umpire said. Ted was loose—there was no question about it.

Ted faced A's pitcher Dick Fowler and smacked a sharp single into the outfield. He was over .400 again. Before the end of the first game of the doubleheader, Ted had rapped out four hits in five at bats. He had raised his average to .403.

What would you do now? Would you sit out the second game? You have already proven that you have both skill and courage. Why risk your .400 average again?

Once again Red Sox manager Joe Cronin offered his star the chance to sit down to protect the average. You can probably guess what Ted told the manager.

Ted was in the lineup for Game 2. The fans applauded his decision.

They clapped even louder when Ted got two hits in his first three times at bat. His average was now .406. There was no question he would be a .400 hitter now! So, when it was time for him to bat a fourth time, he decided to try something new. He sat down. Ted Williams' sensational season was over.

With a place in history on the line, Ted Williams had decided to face the challenge head on. He had gotten six hits in eight times at bat. He had not only preserved his average, he had raised it. Since Ted Williams batted .406 in 1941, no player in either league has been able to match that feat.

Ted Williams went on to become one of the greatest players of all time. He won the Triple Crown twice (leading the league in batting, home runs and runs batted in during the same year). He finished his career with a .344 batting average and 521 home runs. He even hit a dramatic home run in his final time at bat.

Five years after he retired, Ted Williams was elected to the Baseball Hall of Fame. When Ted rose to receive his Hall of Fame plaque, a big crowd in Cooperstown, New York, stood up with him. It was kind of funny to see a standing ovation for the man who wouldn't sit down! But if anyone deserved it, Ted Williams did. ★

Joe Louis on the Ropes

JOE LOUIS HAD EXPECTED BILLY CONN TO
put up a good fight—but not this good! As the bell sounded to start
the 13th round in their heavyweight title boxing match on June 18,
1941, Joe was sure of two things. One was that Billy was winning the match.
The second was that Joe would have to knock out his opponent in order to
keep his boxing title. If both men were standing at the end of the 15th round—
in other words, if the winner had to be decided by adding up the three judges'
round-by-round scores—Billy was going to be the new Heavyweight Champion of the World.

The heavyweight champion is usually considered the strongest and best
fighter in the world. The title had belonged to Joe Louis for exactly four years,
ever since he knocked out James J. Braddock in their June 1937 fight. Louis
didn't want to give it up.

During those four years, Joe had taken on 17 challengers. None of the fights
had even been close. Most of the challengers quickly found themselves
flat on their backs in the boxing ring. Joe expected to make Billy Conn victim
Number 18.

ough and cocky, Billy Conn had earned the nickname "Billy the Kid," like the famous outlaw in the Old West. He had battled his way to become the lightheavyweight champion of the world. Since lightheavyweights don't receive as much fame or money as heavyweights, Billy decided to step up in weight class in order to face Joe Louis.

Bigger, taller and stronger than Billy the Kid, Joe outweighed him 200 pounds to 174 pounds. He also had a longer reach. In order to defeat the champ, Billy knew he would have to stay on the move. One advantage of being lighter was that Conn could move more quickly. He planned to strike quickly with combinations of righthand and lefthand punches then moving out of the way before Joe could hit him back.

In previous fights Billy had gotten into trouble when he was hit hard. He would get angry and try to pound his opponent from close range. He had lost several of those fights because he forgot to use his best weapon—his speed. Billy didn't plan to stay close to Joe Louis in this fight. "I'm going to keep on the run," Billy said. "I know I have lost my temper and my head in some fights, but you can bet I won't this time."

Joe's reply to Billy's bragging was one of the most famous quotes in sports history. "He can run, but he can't hide," Joe said.

A crowd of more than 54,000 people jammed New York City's Polo Grounds on June 18, 1941, to see the Louis—Conn fight. More than 6,000 fans had traveled by bus to New York from Pittsburgh, Billy's hometown. They cheered loudly for their hero, whom all the experts said was an underdog.

Despite the loud cheering by the Pittsburgh fans, Billy was totally outclassed by Joe in the first two rounds of the fight. Billy tried to run, but Joe kept catching up to him. When he did, he pounded Billy with some heavy punches. However, Billy was known to be a slow starter in a fight. His fans said that once he warmed up, this was going to be *some* battle.

In Round 3 Billy kept running, but he stopped now and then to land a few punches of his own. One combination was particularly effective. To keep the challenger's fists from making contact, Joe even had to hold onto Billy. He hadn't had to use that tactic in his first 17 title fights! The fans went wild.

In the fourth round Billy kept up his hit-and-run attack and hurt Louis, whose knees buckled after one series of punches. Somehow the champ managed to stay on his feet. Joe came back with some strong shots of his own in Round 5. He staggered Conn. Luckily for Billy, the bell sounded to end the round. Heading toward the wrong corner, the dizzy fighter had to be helped by his trainers.

Billy's strength and speed were back by the time the next round started, and he began to dominate the match. After one hard punch he yelled at Joe, "You've got a fight on your hands this time, Joe!" He didn't have to tell Joe Louis that! Louis was well aware that he had his hands full with the young fighter.

In Round 12 Billy stopped running so much and started puching more. Now Joe became the one trying to "hide." For the first time in nearly five years, the great Joe Louis was in trouble. He survived the 12th round— just barely. Now the crowd was on its feet, sensing a major upset. Two judges had Conn clearly in front in the fight; the third judge thought the fight was tied so far. If Billy could hold on for three more rounds—nine more minutes—he would become the heavyweight champion.

Billy Conn battling the champion, Joe Louis, during their 1941 heavyweight title bout.

Before the 13th round began, Joe's trainer shouted into his ear, "You've got to knock him out to win!" Joe came out of his corner with that idea in mind. As Joe raced toward him, Billy stood his ground. He had decided not to keep his pre-fight promise to use his speed at all times. Just before the round, Billy had told his trainers, "I'm going to knock the bum out." The trainers had tried to change his mind, but they couldn't.

The two fighters began to slug it out in the middle of the ring. Everyone in the crowd was standing and shouting encouragement to their favorite fighter. For the first two minutes of the round Billy scored well with his punches. Then the tide began to shift Joe's way, and the champ went on the attack.

Near the end of the round, Joe struck Billy with a powerful uppercut to the chin. It snapped the challenger's head back and stunned him. Then the champ moved in "for the kill." With 20 seconds to go in the 13th round, a Louis punch sent Conn toward the mat. Another struck him on the way down.

The referee began the knockdown count at 2:48 of the 13th round. 1... 2...3...4...5...Conn made an attempt to get up. 6...7...8...Billy reached his knees just as the referee shouted "9...10!" The referee signaled the end of the fight two seconds before the end of the round. Just two seconds!

Joe Louis was still the champ. He defended his title many more times before his retirement in 1949, and he didn't lose a single fight. During that winning streak in 1946 he fought Billy Conn one more time. That time, he stopped Conn in the eighth round in a fight that really wasn't close. Many people still consider Joe Louis the best boxer of all time.

Billy Conn knew the secret to beating Joe Louis was to stay on the run. In the end he stopped running and he couldn't hide. "I guess maybe I had too much guts and not enough common sense," Billy said later.

When the pressure was greatest and Joe Louis was "on the ropes," he came through like a true champion. ★

FLYING DOWN THE MOUNTAIN

PICTURE THIS. YOU ARE SKIING DOWN A mountain as fast as you can go. Straight down. If you were wearing a speedometer on your skies, the needle would point to 60 miles per hour or faster. The cold wind is whipping against your face; your icy breath fogs up your goggles. Each bump on the mountainside throws you a little off balance, until you fear that you might fall and break your leg—or worse. Still you push yourself to go even faster. Every tenth of a second counts. Your nerves must be as icy as the wind. You want to be an Olympic champion.

That's what it was like for Franz Klammer of Austria as he raced down a mountain in Innsbruck, Austria, on February 5, 1976, during the Winter Olympics. Franz was the 15th skier to head down the downhill course that day, but to most of the Austrian fans watching the race, he was the only one they had come to see.

It's great to be the fastest skier in Austria. It's also pretty rough. People expect you to win every time you enter a ski race. In Austria skiing is the most important sport. Football, baseball or basketball players are heroes in the United States. Skiers are heroes in Austria. Austria's top skier in the mid-1970s—and Number 1 in the entire world—was Franz Klammer. Talk about pressure!

Franz Klammer of Austria during his electrifying downhill run at the 1976 Winter Olympic Games in Innsbruck, Austria. His gold medal thrilled the hometown crowd.

Franz did not let down his fans very often. During the 1975 skiing season, when Franz was just 21 years old, he had entered nine World Cup downhill races and had won eight of those races. All of that success put added pressure on Franz to win at the Olympics, particularly because the Games were being held in his country.

To win or lose the race, Franz would have only one run down the mountain. He would have to go all out from the top of the mountain to the bottom. The course at Innsbruck was a challenging one. The skiers had to travel straight down for nearly two miles. The top of the course was incredibly steep, and there were several fast dropoffs along the way.

Downhill racers must have excellent technique to survive a course like the one in Innsbruck. They must bend into a deep crouch for balance, and lean far forward and hold their poles straight behind them to cut down on wind resistance. The most important thing is speed, and there's no room for error. Racers throw themselves through the air on drop-offs and turn on the very edges of their skis to avoid bumps. All of this may sound pretty dangerous—and it is!

Because Franz had drawn the 15th position, he had to watch some of the world's other great skiers race before him. There were Bernhard Russi of Switzerland, the 1972 Olympic gold medalist, and his countryman Philippe Roux; Herbert Plank of Italy; Ken Read of Canada; and Andy Mill of the United States. Franz watched as all of these men had excellent runs down the dangerous mountain.

As Franz stepped toward the starting gate, he was aware that Russi was the current leader. The Swiss champ had traveled the course in just over 1:46 seconds, more than 65 miles per hour! Could Franz beat that time—or would Russi win his second straight gold medal?

When the starting bell sounded, Franz literally jumped from the gate. His skis barely seemed to touch the ground. He weaved his way through the flags that marked the downhill course. Franz's time was announced at various points along the course.

The crowds along the course and at the bottom became concerned as they listened to those announcements. After two thirds of the race Franz was more than two-tenths of a second behind Russi's pace. It looked like he was going to be the silver medalist. That just wasn't good enough for the Austrian fans.

Sensing that he was behind, Franz bent even lower and made his turns even sharper. Rather than bite his edges into the snow on the turns, he lifted his skis for added speed—which meant added danger. "I thought I was going to crash all the way," he later told reporters.

In the last 1,000 meters of the race, Franz fought the course with all his might. He hit the final straightaway and poured it on even stronger as he neared the end. Crossing the finish line, Franz threw his hands up in triumph. He didn't need to wait for his final time to be announced. He knew he had won; soon the crowd knew too. One minute, 45.73 seconds—nearly one-third of a second faster than Russi!

Franz Klammer had his gold medal. "Now I've got everything. I don't need anything else," he said. Austrian fans had both a hero and an Olympic champion to cheer. As far as they were concerned, that was the way it should be! ★

Montana to the Rescue

HOW CAN YOU TELL IF A FOOTBALL QUARTERBACK is great? Answer these questions: Does he panic when the pressure is on? Can he push his team to a come-from-behind victory? Can he lead a game-winning drive in the closing minutes? No National Football League quarterback has done these things better than Joe Montana of the San Franciso 49ers. Montana led the Niners to four Super Bowl victories between 1982 and 1990. Two of those wins were come-from-behind. But his most famous game-winning drive did not occur during a Super Bowl. It came at the end of the National Football Conference (NFC) championship game in January 1982. That game marked the beginning of the "Montana legend."

There was a lot of pressure on Joe in his first NFC championship game. He had been the starting quarterback for San Francisco for only one and a half seasons. The 49ers were playing one of the most experienced teams in football, the Dallas Cowboys. San Francisco had a better record than Dallas during the 1981 season, but the Cowboys had played in many more big games over the years. They were used to pressure. Dallas had won four NFC titles and had played in four Super Bowls. San Francisco had never won a league title in the team's 35-year history.

San Francisco jumped out to a quick 7-point lead on a touchdown pass from Montana to wide receiver Freddie Solomon in the first quarter. Then Dallas came back with 10 points of its own to take the lead as the period ended. The Niners leaped ahead again in the second quarter on another Montana touchdown pass. But Dallas quarterback Danny White brought his team back into the lead before halftime.

The pattern continued in the third quarter, with San Francisco taking the lead again. The Dallas team's experience seemed to show as the game wore on. San Franciso didn't have much trouble moving the ball against the Dallas defense, but the Niners kept making silly errors. Montana threw three interceptions, and the running backs fumbled three times. Those six errors helped keep Dallas in the game. Then in the last period, Dallas made two solid drives for 10 more points and a 27–21 lead.

Less than five minutes remained in the game when Joe and the Niner offense came back onto the field. The ball was on their own 11-yard line. San Francisco had to go 89 yards for a touchdown in order to win the game. That was when "The Drive" began.

Joe seemed very confident in the team huddle. He made his team-

mates feel more positive too. Joe and head coach Bill Walsh decided to change their normal strategy. The Niners usually passed on most plays. This time, with the Cowboys expecting passes, they ran the ball. San Francisco running back Lenvil Elliot carried the ball several times. Then the Niners called for a trick play. Joe took the handoff and gave the ball to Elliot, who started to run around right end. As the Dallas tacklers closed in on Elliot, he handed the ball to wide receiver Freddi Solomon who was heading in the opposite direction. The double-reverse worked beautifully. Solomon gained 14 yards from the Dallas 49 to the 35.

Those running plays gained a lot of yards, but they took up a lot of time too. Less than three minutes remained in the game, and the 49ers were still a good distance from the end zone.

On the next play the Cowboys were looking for another run. So Montana crossed them up. He threw the ball to Solomon for 12 more yards to the Dallas 23. The Niners gained only 5 yards on the next two plays, and faced a crucial third-down-and-5 situation. However, a Dallas offside penalty gave San Francisco another first down. It was just the break they needed.

The Niners advanced the ball to the eight-yard line. There was now less than a minute to go in the game. Behind by six points, the Niners needed a touchdown and extra-point conversion to win. A field goal would be meaningless. It was third down. If Dallas could stop the next two plays, it would probably win the championship and the right to play in Super Bowl XVI.

Joe refused to panic. With the noise of the home-crowd fans humming in his ears, Montana gathered his teammates in the huddle and called for the next play—a rollout pass. It was a gutsy call. Almost all of the responsibility for making it work would be Joe's. He would take the ball and roll out toward the right

Receiver Dwight Clark gathering in the Joe Montana pass that tied the game late in the fourth quarter of the 1982 NFC championship game. The extra point gave the 49ers a berth in Super Bowl XVI.

side. Then he would look for a pass receiver in the end zone or run the ball himself. The Cowboys defenders wouldn't be sure whether to look for a pass or a run.

As Joe took the snap from center and ran to his right several Dallas linemen chased him. Joe looked first for Freddie Solomon, but he was covered. As the linemen drew closer, Joe spotted Dwight Clark behind two defenders at the back of the end zone. Clark had been moving back and forth in the end zone, trying to get free. Running hard, Joe zipped the ball while off balance toward Clark, arcing it above the heads of the defenders. The pass was perfect, and so was the catch. Clark leaped up to grab it for the score. Only 51 seconds were left in the game. The score was tied, 27–27!

Seconds later Ray Wershing kicked the extra point to give San Francisco a 28–27 lead. Dallas was left with no time to even get into field-goal position. Joe Montana had engineered a great drive when the pressure was on. San Francisco was the new NFC Champion! The Niners went on to win Super Bowl XVI with a 26–21 victory over the Cincinnati Bengals,

the AFC champs. Montana, turning in another stellar performance, was named the game's most valuable player.

Joe Montana added to his legend seven years later during Super Bowl XXIII in January 1989. With a little more than three minutes to go in the game, the Cincinnati Bengals kicked a field goal to take a 16–13 lead. After the kickoff the Niners had the ball on their own eight-yard line. It was up to Joe to lead his team on another long drive for a game-tying field goal or a game-winning touchdown.

This drive featured all passes. Joe called nine pass plays and completed eight. The last pass came with only 34 seconds remaining in the game. The pass to end John Taylor went for 10 yards and gave San Francisco another Super Bowl victory. Joe Montana had come to the rescue again.

As the San Francisco drive began one Cincinnati player had commented, "We've got them now." A teammate replied, "Not really. Have you taken a look at who's quarterbacking that team?" That quarterback was Joe Montana, one of the greatest ever. ★

LAST-MINUTE LUCK

The Lakers vs. the Knicks.

Sometimes you do all the right things, make all the right moves, play as well as you can, but you lose because the other guy gets a couple of lucky breaks. At other times your team is trailing and it lookes like you'll never catch up—until your luck suddenly turns. Or does it? Is it really luck or skill, guts and determination all coming together in the crunch that saves the day? Read the next section and see what you think. ★

BILL BUCKNER'S BUNGLE

*B*EFORE THE 1986 SEASON THE ADVERTISING agency for the New York Mets came up with a new slogan: "New York Mets—The Magic Is Back!" That agency should have gone into the fortune telling business because the 1986 season truly was magical for the Mets. They ran away with the pennant in the National League East Division. Against the Houston Astros in the National League Championship Series, the Mets made several magical comebacks to defeat Houston in six games. That put New York into the World Series against the Boston Red Sox.

However, the Mets magic seemed to have run out in the 10th inning of Game 6 of the World Series. Leading the series three games to two, the Red Sox had also scored twice in the top of the tenth inning of Game 6 to take a 5–3 lead. The Sox needed just three more outs to win their first world championship since 1918.

Wally Backman and Keith Hernandez of the Mets made two outs. Now the Sox needed just one more. Some of the Boston players began celebrating in their dugout. Why not? The team's relief ace, Calvin Schiraldi, a former Mets player, was certain to get one of his old teammates out quickly and end the game.

ets catcher Gary Carter was the next batter. Already suffering from injuries, Carter was also in a hitting slump. He seemed a good bet to make the last out. Although he swung weakly at the first pitch for a strike, he slapped the next pitch into leftfield for a single. Big deal, Sox players and fans thought. Even if Carter scored, Boston would still win by one run.

Normally, power hitter Darryl Strawberry would have been up next for the Mets. He was a real threat to hit a home run to tie the game, but Strawberry had been taken out of the game earlier for a defensive replacement. That meant rookie Kevin Mitchell was the next batter. Acting more like a veteran than a rookie, he punched a single right up the middle. Now there were two men on base, and the fans in New York's Shea Stadium were going wild.

Ray Knight was up next. Schiraldi got two quick strikes on the Met third baseman. Before Schiraldi could put a third strike over the plate, Knight hit the Mets third straight single to the outfield to drive home a run. The score was now 5–4, and the tying run was on third base. The winning run was on first.

Tension was building in the Red Sox dugout. Boston fans were beginning to sweat. They were remembering all the times in the past when the

Red Sox had come close to a championship but had failed in the end. Maybe they thought about Enos Slaughter's mad dash that helped St. Louis dump the Red Sox in the 1946 World Series (see pages 31-34). Or perhaps they remembered Bucky Dent's clutch homer in the 1978 playoff with the Yankees that ended another Boston pennant run (see pages 7 -11). In any case, they were worried—very worried.

Boston manager John McNamara decided it was time to change pitchers. He brought in veteran reliever Bob Stanley to put out the Mets fire. The first man Stanley faced was outfielder Mookie Wilson.

Stanley's best pitch was a sinkerball. The pitch would start out waist high, then dip down just as it reached the plate. Stanley's sinkerball was a very hard pitch to hit. It was also difficult for a catcher to handle, particularly if it fell to the ground before it reached home plate.

After four pitches to Wilson the count stood at two balls and two strikes. Stanley then threw four straight sinkerballs to try to strike out Wilson. The Mets batter fouled off each one; the tension was really building now.

Stanley's next pitch, another sinkerball, was an inside fastball—so far inside that Wilson had to do a little dance to get out of the way. The ball sailed past Boston catcher Rich

Bill Buckner scrambling for the Mookie Wilson ground ball that went through his legs and allowed Ray Knight to score the winning run in Game 6 of the 1986 World Series.

Gedman and went all the way to the backstop.

By the time Gedman had retrieved the ball, Kevin Mitchell had raced home with the tying run and Ray Knight had advanced to second base. Now the winning run was in scoring position.

Stanley threw one more sinkerball and Wilson hit a slow-rolling grounder toward first base. It was an easy out for Boston first baseman Bill Buckner to make. "Billy Buck" was a tough veteran player, but he was suffering from injuries to his legs, and could barely walk. Buckner limped toward the ball and bent down to pick it up. But the ball went right through his legs!

Knight raced home with the winning run. The World Series was tied at three games apiece. The magic was back! Bill Buckner's bungle had given the Mets a second chance to win the World Series.

Two days later the teams squared off for the seventh and deciding game. Boston got off to a quick 3–0 lead. Then the "Mets Magic" took over again. In the sixth inning, Keith Hernandez doubled with the bases loaded to drive in two runs. Then a bloop shot to rightfield by Gary Carter brought in the tying run. A Ray Knight homer broke the tie during the next inning.

The Mets extended their lead to 6–3. Boston made a comeback, but they ended up one run short. The final score was 6–5, Mets. Boston still didn't have its World Series banner. Red Sox fans blamed bad luck and Buckner's bungle. Maybe they should have put the blame on the magician who cast a spell over the New York Mets in 1986! ★

SHOWDOWN IN MIAMI

HAVE YOU EVER SEEN ONE OF THOSE OLD western movies, the kind in which two gunfighters face off against each other in an exciting showdown? The gunfighters draw their guns and begin firing. One falls, while the other walks away victorious.

A showdown that seemed a lot like one from the old West took place on the afternoon of November 23, 1984, in Miami's Orange Bowl stadium. In this case the two gunfighters were really "pass-slingers." They were Doug Flutie of the Boston College Eagles and Bernie Kosar of the University of Miami Hurricanes, two of the top passers in college football history.

The B.C.–Miami game was billed in television and newspaper ads as "The Battle of the Quarterbacks." The showdown between Flutie and Kosar started right at the beginning of the game. The quarterbacks led their teams up and down the field to score. At the end of the first quarter, Boston College led 14–7. At the half the Eagles lead was 28–21. Forty-nine total points, and it was only halftime! The fans figured there would be even more fireworks in the second half. They were right!

In the third quarter the two teams slowed down slightly. B.C. kicked a field goal, while Miami added a field goal and a touchdown. That made the score 31–31 at the end of three quarters.

B.C. broke the tie with a field goal early in the final period. Then it was the Hurricanes turn to strike Kosar handed the ball to running back Melvin Bratton at Miami's 48-yard line. Bratton didn't stop running until he had crossed the goal line 52 yards away for a touchdown. Now Miami was leading for the first time, 38–34.

Flutie wasn't about to give up. He directed a solid Eagle drive that ended with a one-yard touchdown plunge by Steve Strachan. Now B.C. was on top again, 41–38.

That wasn't the end, however. Kosar knew there was time for one more drive; Miami wanted to accomplish two things on the drive. The Hurricanes wanted to score the winning touchdown, and they wanted to use up as much of the remaining time as possible. The way Flutie was playing, he would need only a few seconds to find a way for his Eagles to score.

As Miami moved down the field toward the B.C. goal line, Kosar's passing was right on target. With just 28 seconds left, Melvin Bratton scored his second touchdown of the day on a short run to put Miami in front, 45–41. Some disappointed Boston College fans began to edge toward the exits. They didn't want to be around to witness a Miami celebration. But before they left the Orange Bowl, many of the fans turned around to watch Doug Flutie try one more time.

The Miami kickoff used up four

precious seconds, so the ball was on the Boston College 20 with 20 seconds to go. Several quick Flutie passes brought the ball just over midfield. There was time for only one more play. Everyone watching the game at home or in the stadium knew what was going to happen next. Flutie was going to send his receivers down to the goal line as fast as they could go before heaving the ball with all his might toward the end zone. He hoped for one of three things to happen. Either a B.C. receiver would catch the ball outright, a Miami defender would tip the ball and a B.C. receiver would catch it, or a Miami defender would cause pass interference and the ball would be placed on the one-yard line with B.C. given one more play to score.

Flutie dropped back, and the Hurricanes defensive linemen put on a hard rush. The huge linemen dwarfed the 5′9″ quarterback and blocked his view of his receivers. But Flutie didn't need to see; he just needed to throw. He did.

The ball went in a high arc. It seemed to stay up in the air for an unbelievably long time. Meanwhile the game clock had run out. This was positively the last play. At the other end of the pass, in the end zone, wide receiver Gerard Phelan was standing in the middle of several Miami defenders.

At just the right instant, Phelan

jumped as high as he could. He grabbed the ball over the outstretched arms of the Miami players and fell backwards into the end zone. Touchdown! B.C. won, 47–45!

Doug Flutie's teammates mobbed him and lifted him onto their shoulders. The 5′9″ quarterback had stood up to Florida pass-slinger Bernie Kosar and had beaten him in the showdown. And what a showdown it was!

Both quarterbacks had outstanding days. Flutie completed 34 of 46 passes for 472 yards and 3 touchdowns. Meanwhile Kosar had 25 completions in 38 attempts for 447 yards and 2 TDs. "The Battle of the Quarterbacks" turned out to be just that. It was a lot more exciting than an old Western movie! ★

THE STEELERS "STEAL" A WIN

PITTSBURGH STEELERS OWNER ART ROONEY WAS feeling pretty sad. A few minutes before, Rooney had been on top of the world. His team had been leading the Oakland Raiders, 6–0, in a first-round American Football Conference playoff game in December 1972. When Oakland's backup quarterback, Ken Stabler, had turned a Raider mistake into a touchdown, Rooney's guys were suddenly behind, 7–6. Only a minute remained in the game. The Steelers had the ball, but they didn't seem to be getting anywhere. It looked like the Raiders were sure to win.

Rooney stood up in his special owner's box in Pittsburgh's Three Rivers Stadium. Boarding an elevator to take him down to the Steelers locker room, he wanted to go there to congratulate his players on their fine season and to tell them how sorry he was that they had lost. While Rooney was on the elevator, he didn't see what was happening on the field. He didn't hear all the cheering by the Pittsburgh fans either. He missed one of the most amazing plays in pro football history—and one of the most controversial too.

he story really began almost a year earlier when the Steelers had chosen Penn State fullback Franco Harris in the first round of the 1972 college draft. Harris had spent much of his college career blocking for halfback Lydell Mitchell. But the Steelers believed he would make both a powerful runner and a good pass receiver in the pros.

In his first year in the NFL, Franco rushed for more than 1,000 yards, caught 21 passes and scored 11 touchdowns. Named the league's "Rookie of the Year," he also led Pittsburgh to its first winning season in nine years and its first playoff berth in more than a decade.

Franco, quarterback Terry Bradshaw and defensive lineman "Mean" Joe Greene helped turn the Steelers into one of the top teams in the league.

The Steelers-Raiders game was a tight defensive struggle. Neither team scored during the first half. In the third quarter Pittsburgh drove deep into Raider territory but had to settle for a short field goal. That made the score 3–0. Another field goal midway through the fourth quarter gave Pittsburgh a 6–0 lead.

The "miracle catch," part one: The football is suspended in the air after touching defender Jack Tatum (#31). John "Frenchy" Fuqua (#33) was the intended receiver.

The "miracle catch," part two: Franco Harris grabs the loose ball and begins his scamper downfield for the game-winning touchdown.

Meanwhile the Raiders were having a lot of trouble on offense. Oakland coach John Madden decided to replace his starting quarterback, Daryle Lamonica, with backup Ken Stabler. That turned out to be a good move. Stabler led a Raider drive in the closing minutes of the game. With the ball on the Steeler 30-yard line, Stabler called for a handoff. Somehow the quarterback and the running back got their signals crossed. Stabler found himself all alone in the backfield. He decided to run with the ball himself. He outran the Pittsburgh defenders all the way to the end zone for a Raider touch-

down. George Blanda's extra point put Oakland up for the first time all day, 7–6.

Only 1 minute and 13 seconds were left in the game when Oakland kicked off to Pittsburgh. Bradshaw tried several pass plays that gained little yardage and used up most of the remaining time. Things looked pretty bleak for the Steelers. That's when Mr. Rooney decided to head down to the locker room.

Only 22 seconds remained. Pittsburgh had the ball on its own 40-yard line on fourth down. Not only did the Steelers have to make a first down, but also they had to get close enough to try a field goal to win the game. Bradshaw went back to pass. He barely avoided a Raider lineman who tried to tackle him. Then he spotted halfback John "Frenchy" Fuqua at the Oakland 35-yard line and threw the ball toward him. Oakland defensive back Jack Tatum saw where the pass was headed, and he raced toward Fuqua. Tatum and the ball arrived at exactly the same second. The ball deflected off either Fuqua or Tatum. The ball then headed straight back toward Bradshaw.

Franco Harris had also been watching the play closely. When he saw Bradshaw's pass flying toward Fuqua, he began running that way too. "I wasn't supposed to be there," Franco said later. "In football you're taught to go to the ball. When Terry [Bradshaw] put it in the air, I took off. I figured Frenchy might need a block if he caught the ball."

When the ball was deflected Franco was in perfect position a few yards behind Fuqua and Tatum. He caught it in the air a few inches off of the ground. Then he began streaking toward the end zone. He crossed the goal line to score the winning touchdown with only five seconds left in the game.

The fans cheered loudly as the Steelers danced around the field hugging each other. The Raiders protested loudly. They claimed that

Franco's touchdown should not count. In 1972 there was a rule that an offensive player could not catch a pass that his teammate had tipped. However, it was legal to catch a pass that a defender had touched first. So the question was: Did the ball deflect off of Steeler Frenchy Fuqua or Raider Jack Tatum? Because the referees were not sure, they called on a game official who was stationed in the press box overlooking the field. The official watched the replay on television. Then he gave his opinion—Pittsburgh touchdown!

Franco Harris's amazing catch and run had won the game for the Pittsburgh Steelers. What a way for a rookie to cap a great season!

The celebrations in Pittsburgh didn't last long, however. The next week the Steelers faced off against the Miami Dolphins for the AFC championship. Miami had not lost a game all season and edged Pittsburgh, 21–17, for the Dolphins 16th straight win.

Franco Harris and the Steelers had more great days ahead of them. They won four Super Bowls between 1975 and 1980, more than any other team has. Franco Harris went on to become the third leading runner in NFL history before he retired in the mid-1980s. But nothing in his great career ever topped his unbelievable catch that "stole" a playoff win for the Steelers in 1972. ★

A WONDER FOR THE WOLFPACK

FOR BASKETBALL PLAYER LORENZO CHARLES, everything seemed to be happening in slow motion. The North Carolina State forward was standing near his team's basket. As his teammates Dereck "Whitt" Whittenburg and Sidney Lowe dribbled out the remaining seconds of the game, he waited for one of them to shoot the ball... and waited. Lorenzo didn't look up at the clock. He knew that less than 10 seconds remained in the biggest game of his life. He waited and watched the ball. That was his job. Five seconds were left. Whit let fly an impossible shot from what seemed like the next town—at least 35 feet away. Lorenzo knew that the ball wasn't going to reach the basket. He had to get to it... and fast!

In 1983 no one dreamed that Lorenzo Charles or his North Carolina State Wolfpack team would be playing in the NCAA basketball championship game. Even fewer people thought the Wolfpack would be in a position to actually win the game, but Coach Jim Valvano's N.C. State team could win—if Lorenzo could get that ball flying toward the basket. It had been a roller coaster year for the Wolfpack. They started out the season winning, but Whittenburg, the heart of the team, had broken an ankle. While Whitt was out of the lineup, the team's record fell to nine wins and seven losses.

When Whittenburg came back, N.C. State began an unbelievable run at the college championship. The team had two secret weapons. The first was the team's guards. They were terrific outside shooters. The second weapon was Coach Valvano's fouling strategy. In close games, he would have his players foul the other team's poor foul shooters. If the opponents sank both foul shots, N.C. State could still come back downcourt and sink a two or three-point basket of its own. If the opponents missed, N.C. State had control of the ball and a chance to pick up two or three points.

Still, the Wolfpack lost a total of ten games during the season—too many for them to be picked to play in the NCAA tournament. The only way they were going to get into the college basketball playoffs was by winning the Atlantic Coast Conference (ACC) tournament. To win they were going to have to beat two highly ranked teams—North Carolina, led by Michael Jordan, and Virginia, led by Ralph Sampson.

N.C. State played North Carolina in the ACC semifinals. Although North Carolina was up by six in the second half, the Wolfpack's three-pointers and fouling strategy helped the team pull off an upset. In the finals against Virginia, the nation's Number 1 team, N.C. State held on to a small lead. The Wolfpack won the championship and a berth in the NCAA tournament.

N.C. State almost didn't make it past the first round! Playing against Pepperdine, they were down 59–55 with 30 seconds to go in overtime. Pepperdine had the ball, and they kept it in the hands of their best foul shooter, Dane Suttle. N.C. State had to foul Suttle twice. He missed both times. Each time, N.C. State came back with a basket of its own to tie the score as the overtime ended. State eventually won the game in double overtime.

In the regional finals State faced Virginia. With the game tied near the end, Coach Valvano told his players to use the fouling strategy. They did; Virginia guard Othell Wilson hit one of two free throws. Then the Wolfpack got its chance. Lorenzo Charles was fouled under his basket and sank both free throws. N.C. State won 63–62. The Wolfpack was heading for the Final Four.

After one more victory N.C. State was in the national championship game against a tough team from the University of Houston. The Cougars were such great dunkers that they were called the "Phi Slamma Jamma fraternity." Leading the way for Houston were Clyde Drexler and Akeem "The Dream" Alajuwon, both of whom became NBA stars.

People began comparing this final

73

Lorenzo Charles, looking as shocked as everyone else in the arena, moments after stuffing the ball through the hoop. The surprise basket gave the underdog Wolfpack of North Carolina State the 1983 NCAA title.

game to the battle between David and Goliath. The University of Houston—"Goliath"—was expected to win the fight with little effort.

Houston got out to a lead in the first half. Then the Wolfpack made a comeback. Hitting lots of three-pointers, N.C. State opened up an eight-point advantage. But the Cougars raced back. Using its running and jamming game, Houston out-scored State 17–2. The Cougars were now ahead, 52–45. For some reason Houston Coach Guy Lewis ordered his players to slow the game down. They held the ball instead of shoot-ing it. A few steals by State players helped the Wolfpack score 7 straight points to tie the game at 52. Less than two minutes remained.

Coach Valvano didn't want Hous-ton to control the ball and get the last shot. So he ordered his players to foul Houston freshman Alvin Frank-lin, who had not taken a foul shot all night. When Franklin missed, N.C. State had the ball and a chance to pull off the upset of the century.

The final seconds ticked off as State's Dereck Whittenburg and Sid-ney Lowe dribbled. Lowe tried to set up a final shot, but the ball was knocked away. Whittenburg recov-ered it, but he was nearly 35 feet from the basket with three seconds to go in the game. Whitt took one step forward and let the ball fly.

Everyone in the arena held his breath and watched the ball follow a rainbow path toward the basket. Only Lorenzo Charles seemed to know where the ball was heading. Realizing that it was going to fall short, he leaped, grabbed the ball and slammed it through the hoop just as the final buzzer sounded.

For a few seconds the crowd sat in stunned silence. Then Coach Valvano jumped high in the air and raced onto the court, hugging and kissing everyone he saw. N.C. State had won the NCAA championship in an amazing upset. David had beaten Goliath once again. ★

THE WILD, WILD WEST

THE NEW YORK KNICKERBOCKERS PLAYED THE Los Angeles Lakers in the final round of the 1970 National Basketball Association playoffs. The Knicks won Game 1. The Lakers won Game 2. Then came Game 3. First the Knicks won that game, then the Lakers won that game. Then the Knicks. Then the Lakers. Then . . .

You get the picture. Game 3 was pretty remarkable. In the closing seconds the lead kept switching from team to team. One thing was clear: Whichever team could get off the last shot was going to win the game.

The Lakers were used to playing in the final round of the playoffs. They had reached the finals five times during the 1960s. Each time their opponents had been the Boston Celtics, and they had never been able to top the Celtics for the NBA title. For Laker star Jerry West that was very frustrating. He really wanted to play on a championship team before he retired. West was sure that 1970 was going to be the Lakers' year.

wo of the reasons West was so sure were his teammates. The 1970 Lakers had the greatest offensive player in basketball history, center Wilt Chamberlain. They also had forward Elgin Baylor, a super-scorer and passer. Chamberlain had been traded from the Philadelphia 76ers to the Lakers midway through the 1968–69 season. When Chamberlain first joined West and Baylor in Los Angeles, basketball experts predicted that L.A.'s "Big Three" would never be able to play well together. Each one was too interested in being the star, the experts said. That was true during their first season together. But Wilt changed his game completely in 1969–70 by concentrating more on passing and defense and less on scoring. The Lakers became an outstanding team.

The Knicks were much younger and much less experienced than the Lakers. Although none of the Knicks had ever been in the NBA finals before, they were one of the most balanced teams in NBA history. The Knicks played "smart" basketball. Willis Reed was the big man in the middle on offense and defense; forward Dave Debusschere concentrated on rebounding. Guards Walt Frazier and Dick Barnett and forwards Bill Bradley and supersub Cazzie Russell handled most of the outside shooting.

The Knicks–Lakers Series went all seven games and featured some incredibly dramatic moments. But no other game could compare to Game 3.

The game was held in Los Angeles where the hometown crowd was excited and loud. With their fans cheering them on, the Lakers jumped out to a 14-point lead by halftime, 56–42. In the third quarter, however, the Knicks seemed to hit every shot they took from the outside. The Laker lead began to disappear.

In the fourth quarter, New York came within one point of the Lakers. Then L.A. had a scoring spurt of its own and stretched the lead back to seven. The Knicks made another surge to tie the game at 97 with 50 seconds to go. A foul shot by Willis Read broke the tie. New York was ahead for the first time all night, 98–97.

The Lakers worked the ball around and used up nearly all of the 24-second shot clock. With only 38 seconds left in the game, West hit a jump shot to put L.A. back on top. Lakers fans were certain that was the winning shot.

The Knicks raced the ball upcourt. Dick Barnett took a shot from the deep corner. *Swish!* New York was back in front.

Los Angeles called its final timeout to set up what they hoped would be

Jerry West making a spectacular shot.

the last play of the game. Before the play could really get started, Barnett fouled Wilt Chamberlain. That was a good play on the part of the Knicks. Wilt was one of the worst foul shooters in the league. He continually clanked the ball off the rim or backboard and seldom through the net. His first shot was a "brick." However, Wilt sank the second free throw to tie the game. Now there were 13 seconds left.

The Knicks worked the ball inside, and DeBusschere hit a short jumper to put New York ahead by two with only three seconds left. Since Los Angeles had used up its last timeout, the Lakers had to take the ball in from the end of the court, not from half-court. After tossing the ball toward Jerry West, Chamberlain began walking toward the locker room. He didn't really watch as West took three steps forward and heaved the ball up into the air from almost ten feet behind the half-court line. The 63-foot shot went right through the net as the buzzer sounded! The game was tied again.

Chamberlain came back in a hurry as the game went into a five-minute overtime period. As you might have expected, the lead see-sawed back and forth in the overtime. With 1:27 to go, Reed hit a foul shot to put New York ahead, 109–108. Neither team could score again until Dick Barnett hit a jumper with four seconds left. That made the final score New York 111, Los Angeles 108.

For Jerry West the game was yet another frustration. He had played his heart out. He scored 34 points, (including the 63-foot miracle shot), but the Lakers had still lost. Since Los Angeles would eventually lose the series to New York in seven games, Jerry West would have to wait at least one more year to play on a championship team.

You may be happy to know that Jerry did finally earn a championship ring two years later. However, that's another wild story. . . . ★

PULLING TOGETHER

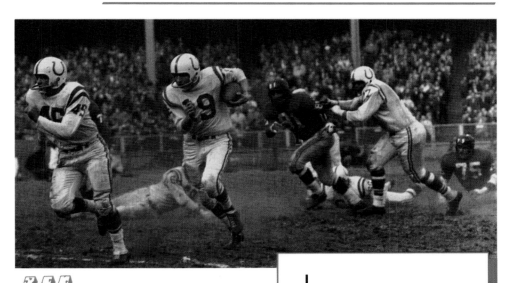

Johnny Unitas of the Baltimore Colts.

*W*hat makes a champion? In individual sports it's the skill, smarts and stamina of a particular player that sets him or her apart from all the rest. But it takes more than one superstar to make a championship team. The players must work together as a unit, supporting and helping each other instead of going for the glory on their own. Read on, and you will discover some exciting examples of the triumphs of teamwork! ★

Magic Johnson moves for the score during Game 6 of the 1980 NBA finals.

A Magic Trick

THE LOS ANGELES LAKERS WERE IN SERIOUS trouble. The Lakers had surprised most basketball experts by making it to the NBA finals in 1980. Now they were leading the Philadelphia 76ers three games to two. If they could win one more game, they would be world champions. All of a sudden their luck seemed to have turned.

The Lakers captain and top scorer was Kareem Abdul-Jabbar, who had been playing brilliantly throughout the playoffs. He had one of his best games in the fifth game of the finals against Philadelphia. Near the end of that game, he sprained his ankle badly. No one was sure whether Kareem would be in the lineup for the rest of the series.

Kareem was the "big man" for the Lakers, both in size and ability. Without his scoring, rebounding and leadership it would be tough for Los Angeles to get past Philly. What was Coach Paul Westhead going to do if Kareem couldn't play?

The big problem was who to put in the middle, at the center position. Westhead had few choices. He could play one of his two power forwards at center. Both Spencer Haywood and Jim Chones had some experience in the middle, but neither had played center much during the year. If Coach Westhead moved them, he might destroy the balance that had kept the Lakers on top most of the season. But what other choice did he have?

The coach shocked everyone, including his team members, when he announced that Earvin "Magic" Johnson was going to play center in Game 6. Although Magic was tall, 6′8″, he hadn't played center since high school. Magic was the team's point guard, the guy who handled the ball and made most of the passes. But he was a rookie! How could he possibly stand up to the pressure of playing a new position in one of the biggest games of the year? Could his teammates give him enough support on defense and offense for L.A. to win the game and the championship?

Magic had been putting up with pressure and with new roles for most of his basketball career. In high school he was one of the top scorers in the entire state of Michigan. He was also a great passer and rebounder. After one of his all-around great games a reporter inter-viewed Earvin Johnson in the team's locker room.

"We've got to find you a nick-name," the reporter said. " 'Dr. J' already belongs to Julius Erving [who played for the 76ers]. 'Big E' already belongs to Elvin Hayes [of the Washington Bullets]. I've got it, we'll call you 'Magic,' " the reporter said. From then on, Earvin Johnson was known as Magic.

In his senior year in high school, Magic dominated his team's offense. But the team wasn't winning. Then his coach asked him not to shoot as much. Magic was told to concentrate on making good passes to his team-mates so that they could score as well. By getting everyone involved in the game, the team would be better, the coach reasoned. Magic agreed with his coach. He changed his style of play, and the team went on to win the state championship.

Two years later, Magic played for another championship. By that time he was a sophomore star at Michigan State University. With Magic still making great passes and several teammates helping with the scoring, Michigan State reached the NCAA finals in 1979. In that championship game, they played the Number One team in the country, undefeated Indi-ana State University. ISU's star was sharpshooting forward Larry Bird.

Magic was asked to change his style again for the final game. Michi-

Magic won two trophies for his 1980 championship playoff efforts—one as a member of the title-winning Los Angeles Lakers and the other for being the playoffs' Most Valuable Player.

gan State needed him to concentrate more on scoring in order to beat ISU. Magic did just that. He poured in a game-high 24 points and added 7 rebounds and 5 assists in the winning effort. After the season Magic decided to accept the Lakers' offer to leave college early and turn professional.

Magic's teams in high school and college had won two championships in three years. Now Magic had a chance to make it three titles in four years, if the Lakers could win one of the two remaining games against Philadelphia. A lot of the pressure would be on him. But a terrific team effort by all of the Lakers was needed to make up for the loss of Kareem.

The sixth game was held in Philadelphia, and the 76ers came out firing. Philly couldn't pull away from the Lakers, even though Kareem wasn't playing. With his teammates' help, Magic played a solid game in the middle on defense. He grabbed several big rebounds and scored well near the basket. The lead see-sawed back and forth throughout the first half; the score at halftime was 60–60.

In the second half, Magic and forward Jamaal Wilkes both went on scoring sprees. Together they led the Lakers to an easy 123–107 victory. The Lakers had shocked Philadelphia and the rest of the country by winning without Kareem and by switching their rookie point guard to center.

By the end of the game here is what Magic had accomplished. He had played 47 of the 48 minutes in the game. He had scored 42 points, grabbed 15 rebounds, made 7 assists, had 3 steals and even blocked 1 shot. Not bad for someone who hadn't played center in several years! Coach Westhead had obviously made the right choice.

Magic won a trophy as the Most Valuable Player in the playoffs. But he was prouder to have a share in another trophy, the one presented to the Lakers as the NBA's championship team. Winning the NBA title wasn't a one-man effort. It took a lot of teamwork—and a touch of Magic. ★

FOOTBALL GROWS UP

SUNDAY AFTERNOONS IN THE FALL MEAN ONE thing to American sports fans today—professional football. Football was not always such a popular spectator sport. It was the NFL title game on December 28, 1958 that changed all that.

The game, which was the Super Bowl of that era, was a classic contest between the terrific offense of the Baltimore Colts and the stingy defense of the New York Giants. It featured a brilliant goal-line stand, clutch field goal kicking, a lucky fumble, a broken leg that may somehow have saved the game, a magnificent drive in the game's last two minutes and the first-ever sudden death overtime period in a championship game. In other words it had everything!

Here's a brief description of what happened during the first 58 minutes of the game. The last two minutes of regulation play and the overtime deserve special coverage.

Defense was the story in the first quarter. Once, the Colts drove as far as the Giants 19-yard line. There, Baltimore kicker Steve Myhra attempted a field goal. Although his kick went wide there was a penalty against the Giants on the play. That gave Myhra a second chance. This time Giants linebacker Sam Huff blocked the kick.

ew York took over and started its own drive downfield. The Colts kept the Giants from scoring a touchdown, but Pat Summerall's field goal put New York on top 3–0 as the quarter ended.

Giants fumbles were costly in the second quarter. Running back Frank Gifford lost the ball twice when he was smashed by Colt tacklers, and each fumble led to a Baltimore touchdown. That made the halftime score 14–3, Baltimore.

In the third quarter the drama really began to build. Colt quarterback Johnny Unitas led his team quickly downfield from their own 37-yard line to the Giant 5-yard line. Another Colt touchdown could have put the game out of New York's reach. Everyone expected the Colts to score. After all, they had not been stopped inside the 10-yard line all year. However the Giants defenders obviously didn't care about that statistic. The Colts tried four different runs to get the ball into the end zone. Not one worked. The Giants defense held the line.

The great goal-line stand by the defense inspired the Giants offensive team, which came *alive*. Two runs brought the ball out to the 13-yard line. Then quarterback Charley Conerly hit pass receiver Kyle Rote with a routine toss. Rote was crushed by a Colt defender on the Baltimore 24,

and he fumbled. New York fullback Alex Webster scooped up the ball and dashed toward the Colt end zone. He made it all the way to the one-yard line before he was caught from behind. That lucky fumble play moved New York 86 yards downfield. Two plays later the Giants scored a touchdown to cut the lead to 14–10.

At the beginning of the fourth quarter the Giants got the ball back and drove for another touchdown. Suddenly they were ahead 17–14; it looked as if they were in control.

The Colts began a drive of their own. From deep in New York territory the Baltimore kicker tried a field goal to tie the game. He missed. The 65,000 fans in New York's Yankee Stadium started to think about what winning the championship would feel like. If the Giants offense could get a few more first downs, New York could run out the clock and win the NFL title.

Then a strange thing happened in the next play, and it turned the whole game around. The Giants had the ball on their own 40 on third down. They needed four yards for a first down. Less than three minutes remained in the game. Quarterback Charley Conerly handed the ball to Gifford, who started out running wide and then cut in toward the middle of the line. Baltimore's outstanding defensive end Gino Mar-

chetti grabbed Gifford near the first down marker. Then the Colts gigantic tackle, fittingly named "Big Daddy" Lipscomb, fell on top of Marchetti. There was a loud cracking sound; Marchetti's leg was broken.

The referee was concerned about Marchetti. He waited until the injured Colt was taken from the field before he placed the ball where he thought Gifford had landed. The Giants insisted that the placement was wrong and that Gifford had gained more yardage. But the referee wouldn't change his mind. He called for a measurement, and the chains were brought out. The ball was inches short of a first down. Amazingly, Marchetti's broken leg might have helped the Colts cause.

New York coach Jim Lee Howell decided his team would punt the ball instead of risking a fourth down run. Giant kicker Don Chandler boomed one to the Colt 14-yard line. Colt quarterback Johnny Unitas had his work cut out for him. With less than two minutes to play in the game, Baltimore was 86 yards away from the Giant's end zone. But no one in the league was better at using the clock and getting a score in the last two minutes of a game than Johnny U. He had two of the finest receivers in football on his team, halfback Lenny Moore and end Raymond Berry.

Moore was fast and smooth. Berry ran perfect patterns, and he caught nearly everything thrown his way.

Here's what the Colt crew accomplished in those two minutes: Unitas threw two incomplete passes. On third down he hit Moore for a first down on the Colt 25-yard line. Two straight completions to Berry brought the ball to the Giants 35. Those plays used up a little more than a minute. The clock read 0:43.

Berry broke to the outside on another pass pattern. Unitas spotted him and put the ball right on the mark, as usual. Berry grabbed it, falling at the Giant's 13. The Unitas-Berry combination had moved the ball 62 yards in only three plays!

Kicker Steve Myhra rushed into the game. The Colts had already missed two field goals so there was a lot of pressure on Myhra. He set up for the kick quickly and got it off in a split second. It was perfect! For the first time in National Football League history a championship game was heading into sudden death overtime. The first team that scored would be the winner.

The team captains came out onto the field for the coin toss to decide which team would get the ball first in the overtime. Johnny U. replaced Colts captain Gino Marchetti, who was lying in pain on the sidelines. (Marchetti refused to be taken to the hospital until the game was over.) Johnny U. called "heads," and the toss was "tails." One writer said later that it was Unitas' last wrong call of the day.

The Giants received the kick and started from their own 20-yard line. They gained four yards on the first two plays. On third down and six, quarterback Conerly went back to pass, but he couldn't spot a receiver. When he tried to run for the first down, he was stopped one yard short. The Giants had to punt.

Now it was Baltimore's turn. L. G. Dupree ran for 11 yards. In order to surprise the Giants and end the game right then, Unitas sent a long bomb toward Lenny Moore, who was streaking toward the Giants end zone. The pass was broken up, just barely, by a Giants defender. A run and a pass to fullback Alan Ameche brought another first down. Ameche's nickname was "The Horse" because of his powerful running, but he was also a fine receiver.

A Unitas-to-Berry pass put the ball in Giants territory. On the next play Johnny U. noticed that Giants linebacker Sam Huff was moving back a little to protect against a pass to Berry. He changed the play at the line of scrimmage and called for a run by Ameche right up the middle to where Huff had been. The Colt fullback gained 23 yards, bringing the ball to the Giants 20. On the Giants eight-yard line Unitas hit Berry again. Now it was first down and goal to go.

The safe thing to do at this point was to keep the ball on the ground. There was a risk of an interception if one of Unitas' passes went off target. Ameche ran for one yard. Then Unitas did the unthinkable. Dropping back to pass, he hit end Jim Mutscheller near the goal line. If the Colt player had fallen backward, he would have scored. Instead he was knocked sideways at the one-yard line. On the next play Ameche powered his way into the end zone. The Colts won, 23–17.

The game was over on the field, but people talked about it for years to come. They discussed Johnny U.'s coolness under pressure and his rocket arm. They discussed Raymond Berry's 12 clutch pass catches, 3 of which had come in overtime. They discussed Ameche's running, Marchetti's broken leg and Steve Myhra's kicking. Also they wondered why the Giants had punted the ball away instead of going for the first down with less than two minutes remaining in the game.

The fact that everyone was talking about it proved one thing: Millions of people had watched the game! Professional football grew up on that winter afternoon in 1958—and it has been growing in popularity ever since. ★

THE MIRACLE ON ICE

PICTURE THIS. THOUSANDS OF PEOPLE ARE STANDING and watching together, waving American flags and counting down from 10 to 0 in unison. 10...9...8...7...6...5...4...3...2...1...0...An explosion of cheers rings out, almost as loud as a rocket blast. An announcer on the television station that is broadcasting the event to the millions of Americans who are watching at home, shouts, "Do you believe in miracles?" Then a wild holiday celebration begins all around the United States. What's going on here? Is this a special space launching at Cape Canaveral? No, it's the end of the most exciting Olympic hockey game in American history.

The date was February 22, 1980. It was already a holiday, Washington's Birthday, but it became even more special. The setting was the ice hockey rink in Lake Placid, New York, the site of the 1980 Winter Olympic Games. The opponents were a very young, very inexperienced hockey team from the U.S. and a very experienced hockey team from the Soviet Union. Nobody gave the Americans much of a chance of winning this game. After all, most of the Soviets had been playing together for at least eight years and had already won Olympic gold medals in 1972 and 1976. The Soviet team was so powerful that it had even defeated a team made up of All-Stars from the National Hockey League in an exhibition game.

The members of the U.S. team, on the other hand, were mostly college players who had been working together for only about six months. Their coach, Herb Brooks, was a tough and demanding leader. He once told his players, "Gentlemen, you don't have enough talent to win on talent alone." So he had drilled them and drilled them through practice after practice. Many of the players didn't like Coach Brooks very much because of his toughness, but they respected him a lot. He stressed the idea of working together as a team, not trying to make great individual plays.

When the Olympics began, the Soviets were ranked Number 1 of the 12 teams in the hockey competition. The Americans were ranked Number 7. One reason for the Americans' low ranking was that they had played the Soviet Union in an exhibition game three days before the Olympics began. The Soviets had won that contest by a whopping 10–3 score.

The players from the U.S. surprised experts and fans alike. They tied a powerful team from Sweden in the closing seconds of their first match. In their second game, the Americans came from behind to defeat Number 2 ranked Czechoslovakia. Then the U.S. swept by Norway, Romania and West Germany to win a place in the medal round. The

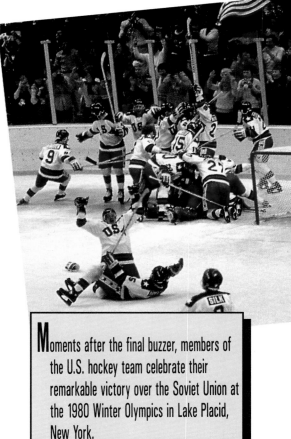

Moments after the final buzzer, members of the U.S. hockey team celebrate their remarkable victory over the Soviet Union at the 1980 Winter Olympics in Lake Placid, New York.

other finalists were Sweden, Finland and the Soviet Union.

The stage was set for a U.S. vs. U.S.S.R. (Union of Soviet Socialist Republics) showdown. At that time in 1980 there were strong anti-Soviet feelings in the United States. The Soviet army had recently invaded the country of Afghanistan, and U.S. President Jimmy Carter had spoken angry words to the Soviet leaders. Lots of the fans in the Lake Placid arena came to cheer for the Unites States and to root against the Soviets. Many carried American flags or wore red-white-and-blue clothes.

The fans were unhappy when the

Soviet Union scored first on a deflected shot that slipped past U.S. goalie Jim Craig. The U.S. tied the score within five minutes only to have the Soviets take a 2–1 lead moments later. Then, with just seconds left in the first period, the first of the day's miracles occurred. An American player took a wild last-second shot that rebounded off the pads of the outstanding Soviet goalie, Vladimir Myshkin. Winger Mark Johnson of the U.S. got to the puck first. He pushed the rebound under Myshkin's pads. The clock read 0:01. The score was tied as the two teams left the ice. Yet things weren't really even. The American players were cheering and hugging each other while the Soviets were upset.

The Soviets scored the only goal in the second period to take a 3–2 lead. Midway through the third period, the U.S. tied the game again. Mark Johnson stole the puck from a defender near the Soviet goal. Then Johnson poked in his second goal of the game. Less than two minutes later, American captain Mike Eruzione, using a Soviet player as a screen, sent a 30-foot slap shot into the Soviet goal. Suddenly the U.S. team was ahead for the first time in the game. The fans went wild. They began chanting, "U.S.A.! U.S.A.!" and "Dee-fense! Dee-fense!"

With minutes left in the game, the Soviets began a powerful attack on the U.S. goal, but Jim Craig was up to the task. He turned away every shot. Some of his saves were spectacular. Somehow the Americans held off the Soviets. During the last 10 seconds of the game television announcer Al Michaels said nothing. He let the audience listen to the fans in the arena counting down from 10 to 0. Then he shouted, "Do you believe in miracles?" Most of those watching the game did believe.

But the U.S. players weren't through making miracles. Two days later they faced a powerful team from Finland in their final game of the Olympics. The Americans knew that if they lost the game to Finland they could still come in third in the hockey tournament. Finland jumped out in front, 2–1, after the first two periods. Then the U.S. team scored three times in the final period to win the game and the gold medal.

At the awards ceremony only captain Mike Eruzione stood on the platform while the national anthem, "The Star-Spangled Banner," was played. Then he invited all his teammates to join him while the crowd cheered its new heroes. The players from the U.S. had learned that Coach Brooks was right: They could succeed if they played together as a team. Each of the 20 athletes had played an important role in creating what has come to be known as "the miracle on ice." ★

HISTORY BEGINS FOR THE ISLANDERS

OR THE FIRST TWO YEARS OF ITS EXISTENCE the New York Islanders hockey team was terrible. The Isles, who started out in 1972, were consistently at the bottom of the National Hockey League standings. They didn't get much respect in the New York area. The New York Rangers were the hometown favorites—not those "distant cousins" who played on New York's Long Island. The Islanders were compared to the New York Mets, who set records for losses and for bumbling in the early 60s. Of course the Mets went on to become world champions in 1969.

A team that finishes at the bottom of the standings does have one advantage. The poorer teams get to pick new players through the draft before the better teams do. So the Islanders began building their team with some of the top young players coming into the league. They acquired an excellent scorer in Billy Harris, a top-notch defenseman in Denis Potvin and a tough, acrobatic goalie in Glenn "Chico" Resch. The Islanders began to improve slowly, and by the 1974–75 season—the team's third year in the league—they were in the Stanley Cup playoffs for the first time. That was the good news. The bad news was that their first-round opponent would be the Rangers. There seemed to be two things that the Islanders couldn't do: They couldn't beat the Rangers (they were 1–14 against them), and they couldn't win the hearts of New York hockey fans. Even though they hadn't won the Stanley Cup since 1940, the Rangers were Number 1 in New York.

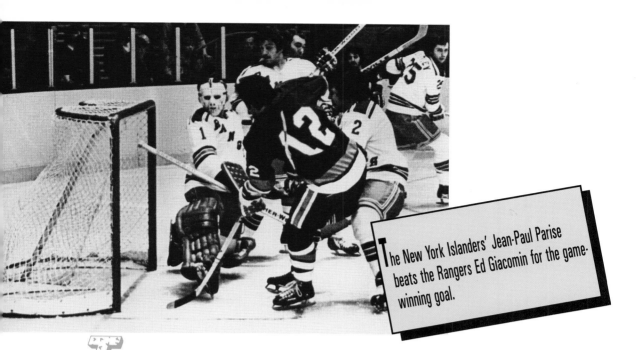

The New York Islanders' Jean-Paul Parise beats the Rangers Ed Giacomin for the game-winning goal.

The first-round playoff between the Islanders and Rangers was a study in contrasts. The Isles were young, inexperienced and generally underpaid. Happy just to be in the hunt for the Stanley Cup, they didn't expect to win. The Rangers were a group of highly paid veterans under real pressure from their fans and the press to win the Cup.

The Rangers weren't particularly worried about their first-round opponent. They figured they would win the best-two-out-of-three play-off against the Islanders in two straight games. As the playoffs began, many Ranger players sported new beards. They vowed not to shave until they won the Stanley Cup.

The first game of the Rangers–Islanders series was held at Madison Square Garden, the Rangers arena.

The Rangers broke out to a 2–0 lead, and their prediction that it would be an easy series seemed correct. Then something strange happened. The Islanders scored once against Rangers goalie Ed Giacomin early in the third period to pull within a goal. Soon they tied the game. Finally they pushed a third shot past Giacomin for the win. Rangers fans were upset, and the players were embarrassed. Meanwhile New York sportswriters didn't know what to make of this unexpected happening.

The second game was played at the Nassau Coliseum, the Islanders home rink on Long Island. This time the Rangers came out shooting and swinging. The Islanders did some swinging of their own, as fights broke out all over the ice. The referee called 50 penalties, a record for a playoff game. The Islanders fought well, but they didn't hold up defensively. The Rangers scored an 8–3 victory. The series was even.

In the third and final game the Islanders took control right away. By the time the third period began they were ahead 3–0. Rangers fans were booing. How could their team be losing to the New York Islanders!

Suddenly the Rangers seemed to remember who they were playing. They couldn't lose to the underdog! The so-called "Broadway Blues" (Broadway is a big street in New York City, and the Rangers uniforms are red, white and blue) made a great comeback. Billy Fairbairn scored a goal. Then Fairbairn and Steve Vickers scored two goals only 14 seconds apart. The game was tied. The score remained 3–3 when the buzzer sounded to end regulation play.

The ice was cleaned, and the two teams took a break before the sudden-death overtime period began. Some of the fans in Madison Square Garden left their seats to get refreshments. Most of them probably wondered when the Rangers were finally going to pull this one out. As it turned out, any fans who didn't hurry back to their seats missed seeing the end of the game!

On the opening face-off the Islanders controlled the puck. A pass went to Jean-Paul Parise, who was standing near the Ranger goal. He flicked the puck past Ed Giacomin. The game was over—in just 11 seconds!

Those 11 seconds were really the start of New York Islanders history. For the rest of the 1975 Stanley Cup playoffs the Isles were amazing. They lost three straight games to the Pittsburgh Penguins in the next round but came back and won the next four to advance to the Cup semifinal round. Once again they lost three straight to the Philadelphia Flyers.

"Now we've got them where we want them," joked one of the Islanders leaders. "We play best when we're down three games to nothing." He was nearly right. The Isles won the next three games to even up the series. However they lost the seventh game, 4–1. In only their third year of existence the Islanders had come within one game of reaching the Stanley Cup finals. Philly went on to win the Cup in 1975, but the Islanders had proved they were Number 1 in New York.

By 1980 the New York Islanders had become not only the best team in New York but the best team in the league. The Isles took home four straight Stanley Cups from 1980 to 1983. They had a chance to tie the all-time record of five straight Cups in 1984, but they were defeated in the finals by the Edmonton Oilers.

Nevertheless the Islanders had moved quickly from being the worst to being the best. And it all started with those 11 seconds of excitement in 1975. ★

WILD AND WOOLY

Boston defeats Cincinnati .

Do you believe that seeing is believing? Have you ever seen something with your own eyes that you couldn't believe? Some games are like that. They're the ones that go down in the record books because what happened was so completely unexpected, so spectacular, so totally crazy that even the fans who were right there watching could hardly believe what they had just seen. Check out this next section, and you'll understand why!

Bill Mazeroski arriving at home plate after hitting his World Series-winning home run.

PIRATE POWER

*T*HE 1960 WORLD SERIES WAS A CLOSE CONTEST—
even though after six games the New York Yankees had outscored the
Pittsburgh Pirates 46–17. Three of the games had been wild and high-
scoring. As you may have guessed, the Yankees won those games. The other
three were tight and low-scoring, and the Pirates won each of those. It was a
classic example of how different teams win in different ways.

The nearly 37,000 fans who packed Pittsburgh's Forbes Field on October
13, 1960, wondered what the seventh game in the Series was going to be like.
The Pirates had not won a World Series since 1909. If they could keep the
Yankees from going wild and scoring a lot of runs, there was a good chance
Pittsburgh could finally come out on top.

The game started out well for Pittsburgh. After two innings the Pirates had a
4–0 lead. Yankees manager Casey Stengel brought in a relief pitcher to replace
starter Bob Turley and then another relief pitcher to replace the first reliever.
Those moves quieted the Pirates bats for a little while.

*I*n the meantime, the Yankees finally broke into the scoring column in the fifth inning on a solo home run by first baseman Moose Skowron. A run-scoring single by Mickey Mantle and a three-run home run by Yogi Berra brought in four more Yankee runs in the sixth inning. Now the Yankees were ahead, 5–4. The fans figured they were in for another wild game, and they were worried. After all, New York had won three games already by scores of 16–3, 10–0, and 12–0. Once the Yankees started scoring they didn't stop!

The Pittsburgh fans became even more concerned when New York added two more runs in the eighth inning to increase its lead to 7–4. Pittsburgh had only six more outs to turn the game around.

They didn't waste any time. Pinch hitter Gino Cimoli quickly singled with a shot into rightfield. Pirates fans began cheering for a big rally. Their cheers turned to groans as the next batter, Bill Virdon, hit a hard grounder at Yankees shortstop Tony Kubek. It looked like an easy double play. But the ball took a crazy hop— and hit Kubek right in the throat. The Yankees shortstop lay in pain on the ground as Cimoli and Virdon ran safely to first and second base. Luck seemed to be on Pittsburgh's side at last.

After Groat singled to drive in one run, making the score 7–5, Casey Stengel brought in another relief pitcher, Jim Coates. There were runners at first and second with no outs. Bob Skinner moved the runners to second and third with a sacrifice bunt. The next batter was Rocky Nelson. He had already hit a two-run homer earlier in the game. Another home run now, and the game would be tied. Nelson just missed his pitch, however, and sent a high fly ball to rightfield for the second out. The runners held at second and third.

Roberto Clemente was up next. Fast and dangerous, Roberto hit a high chopper toward the hole between the first and second basemen. Skowron, the first baseman, got to the ball, but Coates, the pitcher, forgot that he had to cover first base. Clemente outran the Yankee pitcher to the bag, and Virdon scored the second run of the inning to draw Pittsburgh within one 7–6. Now the Pirates had runners on first and third with two outs. Things were really going their way!

Pittsburgh backup catcher Hal Smith came to the plate next. Smith had entered the game as a defensive replacement for Smokey Burgess. He was a good fielder, but only an average hitter. That was too bad because the Pirates needed him to get a big hit.

Casey Stengel came back out to the mound to talk to his pitcher. Coates

was noted for his sinkerball. The Yankees manager told him, "Keep the ball low. Don't give this guy a high pitch to hit." Coates followed his manager's instructions—and Smith promptly sent the next pitch over the leftfield wall! Pittsburgh was back in front, 9–7. They had scored five runs in the eighth inning!

New York Yankees shortstop Tony Kubek after being hit in the throat by Bill Virdon's sharp ground ball in eighth inning. Second baseman Bobby Richardson calls for time.

Now it was up to Pirates pitcher Bob Friend to get the final three outs against the Yankees and end this wild and woolly game. Friend faced only two Yankees and didn't retire either one. Bobby Richardson and Dale Long each hit singles off him. So Pirates manager Danny Murtaugh brought in another relief pitcher, Harvey Haddix. Haddix was greeted by a hard single from Mickey Mantle that scored one run and sent Long to third base with the tying run. The next batter was Yogi Berra. Yogi whacked the ball down to Rocky Nelson at first base. Rocky made a great stop on the ball. If he had thrown to second base, he probably would have started a double play to end the game. Instead Rocky stopped on first to make the easy out. Next he turned toward second to throw Mantle out. Somehow Mickey was able to sneak past him and made it back safely into first. The tying run came across the plate on the play to make the score, 9–9.

In the bottom of the ninth, Pirates hopes were riding on Bill Mazeroski. Maz was one of the finest fielding second basemen in baseball history. But he was not a very good hitter. Bill Terry, the Yankees' fifth pitcher of the day, was facing Maz. Terry's first pitch was low for ball one; Maz got ready for the second pitch.

"On my previous at bat, I over-swung and grounded out," Maz told reporters later. "I wanted to make certain I didn't do the same thing again."

Terry's next pitch came in waist high, and Mazeroski connected solidly. The ball began sailing toward almost the same spot as Hal Smith's home run had in the eighth inning. It went over the fence just as Maz rounded first base. He began leaping wildly into the air and danced all the way around the bases. At third base a crowd of Pirates fans greeted Mazeroski and ran with him to the plate. Maz made certain he stepped on the plate, and then he raced toward the locker room to escape the mob of fans.

For the first and only time in baseball history the seventh game of a World Series had been decided by a home run in the bottom of the ninth inning. It had been a strange game and a strange series. The Yankees had outhit and outscored the Pirates, but they had not won. Bill Mazeroski, the man known for his great fielding, instead became famous for one swing of his bat. And the Pittsburgh Pirates, who had lost three games in the 1960 World Series to Yankees power, won the most important game of all with a power display of their own. It was a finish no one would ever forget! ★

THE ICE BOWL

YOU HAVE PROBABLY HEARD OF THE ROSE BOWL, the Orange Bowl and the Super Bowl. But have you ever heard of the "Ice Bowl?" No, not the ice cream bowl—the "Ice Bowl." That was the nickname given to the National Football League championship game between the Green Bay Packers and Dallas Cowboys on December 31, 1967.

That game deserved its nickname. It was played in Green Bay, Wisconsin, where the temperature was 16 degrees below zero! As if that wasn't bad enough, the wind was also blowing at 15 miles per hour and even stronger at times. At least the players could run around and smash into each other to keep warm. The 51,000 fans sitting and shivering in the stadium were the ones who were frozen solid!.

The Packers and Cowboys had played each other for the league championship the year before as well. That game was held in the Cotton Bowl in sunny Dallas, Texas. The Packers had won a close one, 34–27. The game had gone down to the last minute before it was decided. Packer defensive back Tom Brown intercepted a pass by Cowboys quarterback Don Meredith on the Green Bay two-yard line to halt Dallas final attempt to tie the game. The win had been doubly important. It gave the Packers the league championship, and it also put them into Super Bowl I against the Kansas City Chiefs, champions of the American Football League. Green Bay won that first Super Bowl, 35–10.

The fans hoped this Green Bay–Dallas game would be as close as the last one. They were also wondering if anyone could catch the ball in such cold and icy conditions! The Packers were playing at home, and they were used to the cold. However, the Cowboys trained in Texas where the temperature almost never went below zero. Some fans thought they might not be able to handle the brutal cold.

Just as they had done the year before, the Packers quickly opened up a 14–0 lead. Then the powerful Dallas defense caused Green Bay quarterback Bart Starr to fumble the ball on his own seven-yard line early in the second quarter. Cowboys defensive end George Andrie recovered the ball and ran it in for a touchdown. The score was 14–7, Green Bay. Dallas got the ball back again a few minutes later and drove all the way to the Packer 14-yard line. The cold didn't seem to be bothering their game a bit! The Pack held the line, however, and Dallas had to settle for a field goal. The half-time score was 14–10, Green Bay.

Neither team could get anything going in the third quarter. Both quarterbacks, Starr and Meredith, were having trouble getting a grip on the icy ball. When they were able to get off a pass the wind often blew it off course.

Then early in the fourth quarter,

Dallas ran a trick play. Halfback Dan Reeves took a pitch from Meredith and began running toward the outside. Reeves stopped and heaved a pass downfield. Flanker back Lance Rentzel caught the ball and raced across the goal line for a 50-yard touchdown. Dallas was in the lead for the first time in the teams' two championship games. Could the Cowboys hang on and earn a berth in Super Bowl II?

Gathering his teammates around him, Starr urged them to put on one more great drive to win their fifth NFL championship in seven years. Then the Packers really began to grind out yardage. Seven plays later Green Bay was on the Dallas 30-yard line with only two minutes remaining in the game.

Starr spotted halfback Chuck Mercein on the next play and tossed him a short pass. Mercein grabbed it and bulldozed his way to the Cowboy 11-yard line. Green Bay was close enough for a tying field goal—even in the icy conditions. But Green Bay wanted more than a tie. They didn't want to have to play an overtime period. One play later Mercein took a Starr handoff and ran to the three-yard line. A little over a minute remained in the game.

The Packers tried twice to get the ball into the end zone, but they were stopped one yard short. That left only 13 seconds, and the Packers

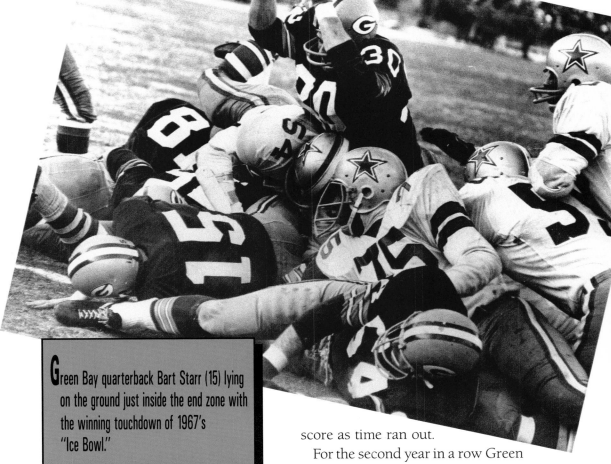

Green Bay quarterback Bart Starr (15) lying on the ground just inside the end zone with the winning touchdown of 1967's "Ice Bowl."

had no more timeouts left. They would have to score on the next play or risk losing the game. There might not be enough time left to get off another play.

Starr decided that he would have to take matters into his own hands. He called a quarterback sneak. That meant Starr would take the ball and head right behind his powerful guard, Jerry Kramer, toward the goal line. He did just that. Kramer and center Jim Ringo opened up a small hole in the Dallas defense, and Starr slipped through for the winning score as time ran out.

For the second year in a row Green Bay had faced a strong challenge from the Dallas Cowboys. And for the second year in a row the Packers had met that challenge. They didn't let the ice or wind or freezing cold beat them.

Two weeks later the Pack topped off its season with a 33–14 win over the Oakland Raiders in Super Bowl II. The game was held in 80 degree weather in Miami, Florida. The Super Bowl probably seemed simple for Green Bay after the "Ice Bowl." This time Packers only had to defeat another football team—they didn't have to worry about getting frostbite too! ★

STOLEN: ONE BALL

SUPPOSE YOU ARE CHOOSING UP SIDES FOR a make-believe Hall of Fame basketball game. You get to pick first.

Do you want the most dominant scorer in the history of pro basketball? Or would you rather select the most dominant defensive player in the history of pro basketball? In other words, would you pick Wilt Chamberlain or Bill Russell?

With Chamberlain you get a man who once averaged more than 50 points and 25 rebounds per game for an entire season! With Russell you get the finest shot blocker and team leader the game has ever had. Either way you're bound to make a good choice.

In the 1960s Chamberlain and Russell were basketball's brightest stars. They had lots of battles against each other, and nearly all of them were fantastic. But none could top the seventh game of the Eastern Division finals in 1965. Russell was playing for the Boston Celtics and Chamberlain for the Philadelphia 76ers.

During the 1964–65 season, the Celtics were big favorites to sweep through the Eastern Division. Everyone expected them to sweep to their seventh straight National Basketball Association championship as well. With Russell in the middle, Tom Heinsohn and Satch Sanders at forward, and Sam Jones and John Havlicek at guard, Boston was loaded with scoring power. The Celts had 62 wins during the regular season, their most ever.

The Philadelphia 76ers finished far behind the Celtics during the season. They ended the year with only a 40–40 record. In this case the statistics didn't tell the whole story. In the middle of the season the 76ers pulled off a big trade with the San Francisco Warriors (who used to play in Philadelphia before they moved west). The trade brought Wilt Chamberlain back to Philadelphia. It took a while for the rest of the 76ers to get used to playing with Wilt. However, by playoff time, Philly was almost Boston's equal. Wilt had lots of support on the 76ers, with Luke Jackson and Chet Walker at forward and Hal Greer and Larry Costello or Al Bianchi at guard.

The Sixers beat the Cincinnati Royals in the first round of the playoffs. That put them into the Eastern Division finals against Boston, and basketball fans were thrilled. Just as everyone had hoped, it would be Russell against Chamberlain. People couldn't wait to see the two stars battle it out!

In Game 1 Russell outrebounded Chamberlain, 32–31. Even though Wilt scored 33 points for Philly, Boston won by 10.

In Game 2 Wilt beat Russell in both rebounding (39–16) and scoring (30–12), and the 76ers won 109–103.

In Game 3 Russell held Chamberlain to only 4 points in the first half. Wilt broke out in the second half, but it was too little, too late. Boston won

112–94.

The hero of Game 4 was Philly guard Hal Greer. With only two seconds left in the game Greer received a long inbounds pass and threw in a 35-foot shot at the buzzer to send the game into overtime. Celtics coach Red Auerbach screamed that the shot had come after time ran out. Boston lost the argument and then the game. So the series was tied 2–2. The tension was really beginning to build.

In Game 5 Russell blocked 12 shots while Wilt scored "only" 30 points. Boston won the game to regain the lead in the series, 3–2.

Boston seemed to have the upper hand in Game 6. In the last quarter, Wilt was called for his fifth foul. One more foul and he would be out of the game. Amazingly enough, Wilt had *never* fouled out of a game in his entire career. He didn't foul out of this one either. He remained aggressive both on offense and defense as the 76ers evened up the series once again with a 112–106 win. Wilt finished the game with 30 points and 26 rebounds.

The seventh game between Boston and Philadelphia was in Boston Garden. The Celtics had history on their side. They had never lost the final game of a series on their home court. They had also won eight straight Eastern Division finals and six straight NBA titles. The 76ers

106

weren't thinking about the past, however. They were out to make history of their own.

Everyone thought the seventh game would come down to the same thing: Chamberlain vs. Russell. They were in for a surprise. Not that the big guys weren't important—but it was someone else who made the biggest play.

After six minutes of play Boston had raced out to an 18-point lead, 30–12. The Sixers slowly fought back into the game. By the third quarter Philly had not only caught up, it had taken the lead, 66–61. Then Boston backup guard K.C. Jones put the brakes on Hal Greer, and the Celts edged back into the lead.

With two minutes to go Boston was up by seven. Chamberlain scored six straight points to pull Philly to within one, but the Sixers now had two problems. Only five seconds remained in the game, and Boston had the ball out of bounds under the Philadelphia basket. All Boston had to do to win the game was to get the ball inbounds and hold onto it for five seconds. It looked like a lost cause for the Sixers.

It was Bill Russell's job to pass the ball in. He saw Sam Jones breaking downcourt and decided to hit him with a one-handed overhead toss. But Russell's pass hit a wire holding up the Philadelphia basket—and fell out of bounds. With five seconds still left on the clock, the ball went back to Philly.

Hal Greer attempted to pass the ball to Chet Walker. Walker was supposed to get the ball to Chamberlain near the basket for a final winning shot or foul or to take the shot himself. Greer lobbed the pass . . . Boston's John Havlicek darted in front of it. He leaped as high as he could and tipped the ball to Sam Jones, who dribbled out the final five seconds. The Boston fans roared with excitement. Celtics' radio announcer Johnny Most began yelling into his microphone, "Havlicek stole the ball! Havlicek stole the ball! Havlicek stole the ball!"

It was an amazing ending. For one of the few times in his career, Bill Russell had made a big mistake. The Celtics had come out on top anyway, thanks to a fast move by John Havlicek. That day Wilt Chamberlain won the battle between the two big men, but Boston won the war— again.

The Celtics went on to defeat the Los Angeles Lakers for their seventh straight NBA title in 1965. However, as far as most fans were concerned, the real championship had already been played and won when John Havlicek stole the ball to save the seventh game against the Philadelphia 76ers. ★

Twelve Innings of Thrills

PETE ROSE OF THE CINCINNATI REDS CAME TO BAT
late in the sixth game of the 1975 World Series. He turned to catcher
Carlton Fisk of the Boston Red Sox and said, "Can you believe this
game!" He couldn't—no one could! The game included some outstanding
clutch hitting, several fine fielding plays and a game-saving throw from leftfield to home plate. The drama continued on into extra innings. Although the
game didn't end until after midnight no one had trouble staying awake! Some
people have even called it the greatest World Series game ever played.

Coming into Game 6 Cincinnati was leading what was already a close and
exciting series three games to two. A win at Boston's Fenway Park would give
the Reds the championship. However, Boston jumped out to a quick 3–0 lead
on rookie Fred Lynn's three-run homer in the first inning. The lead lasted until
the sixth inning when Cincinnati scored three times to tie the game.

he Reds then took a three-run lead of their own in the seventh inning on a Cesar Geronimo home run. Things looked pretty bleak for the home team. Boston fans had suffered through many second-place finishes over the years. They started getting that "runner-up" feeling again.

In the bottom of the eighth the Red Sox got two runners on base. Up stepped pinch hitter Bernie Carbo. Bernie had smashed a three-run homer in an earlier game of the Series. No one in the stands really believed he could do it again, but they kept their fingers crossed anyway. To their surprise and delight, Carbo came through. He hit a shot high into the centerfield stands. The game was tied at 6–6. Boston was still alive, and the fans were on the edge of their seats.

In the ninth inning the Red Sox were on the brink of winning. Second baseman Denny Doyle walked and then went to third base on a Carl Yastrzemski single. There was only one out. Lefthanded relief pitcher Will McEnaney came into the game for Cincinnati. He walked Carlton Fisk to load up the bases and bring up lefthanded hitter Fred Lynn. Red Sox fans loved that move. Lynn was the American League's Rookie of the Year and Most Valuable Player that year. And he had already homered in the first inning. Lynn didn't get his

pitch this time. He lifted a fly ball into shallow leftfield. Doyle decided to test outfielder George Foster's arm. He tagged up and raced toward home plate after Foster made the catch. Foster's throw was perfect, and Doyle was out. The game went into extra innings.

In the 11th it was Cincinnati's turn to threaten on offense, and Boston's turn to make an outstanding defensive play. Ken Griffey reached first on a single. Then Joe Morgan slammed a ball toward the rightfield fence; it looked like a sure double or triple. Everyone thought the speedy Griffey would score easily, but Sox rightfielder Dwight Evans never gave up on the ball. He went all the way back to the fence and made a spectacular leaping catch. Then he fired a rocket shot to first base to throw out Griffey for a double play. Red Sox fans were breathless. (The Reds were pretty stunned too!)

Things got tense again for the Sox in the 12th inning. Tony Perez and George Foster were both on base when slugger Cesar Geronimo came up to bat. The Reds' centerfielder was having a good series. He had already hit a homer in the eighth inning. This time, however, Boston pitcher Rick Wise struck out Geronimo to end the inning safely.

In the bottom of the 12th, the first batter up for Boston was Carlton Fisk. He took the first pitch from

Cincinnati's Pat Darcy for ball one. Then Darcy tried to slip a sinkerball past the Sox catcher. Fisk wasn't fooled—he blasted it toward the left-field stands. It was definitely hit hard enough to be a home run. The only question was whether the ball would stay fair or go foul.

Fisk had moved a few steps away from the plate and was waving his arms toward fair territory. The ball must have listened to him. It hit the screen on the fair side of the foul pole. Two inches farther to the left, and it would have been a strike. But it was a home run! Fisk leaped around the bases, and fans and teammates poured onto the field to congratulate him.

After all that, the Red Sox hadn't even won the World Series—just the sixth game! The next night the Sox and Reds put on another great battle. Boston jumped out in front again, but Cincinnati caught up. In the ninth inning Joe Morgan lifted a single into shallow centerfield. Fred Lynn raced in to get the ball, but he just couldn't reach it. The winning run scored on the play, and Cincinnati won the World Series. Boston was a runner-up again, but they truly deserved to be considered co-champs in 1975. ★

Carlton Fisk connects for his game-winning homer in the bottom of the 12th inning in Game 6 of the 1975 World Series.

SECTION 6

THE DEBATE GOES ON

Eddie Tolan wins the 100-meter dash.

as it a goal or not? Did he win or did he lose? In any sports contest an official has to make the final decision as to who the winner is, even when it seems too close to call. But that doesn't mean that everybody has to agree with him. Far from it! In the following pages you will discover that people have been arguing about the outcome of certain competitions for more than half a century! ★

GOAL OR NO GOAL?

*T*HE RULES IN SOCCER ARE VERY CLEAR. ONE OF them is that the ball must land inside the net and completely behind the goal line to count as a score. Just because the rules are clear does not mean they are always followed, however. Did a mistake help decide the winner in the final game of the 1966 World Cup tournament? Some soccer fans, particularly those from West Germany, still think so. No matter what the answer, that game was one of the most exciting in international soccer history.

Everyone knew there was going to be a World Cup championship competition in 1966. For a while, however, no one was sure there would be a World Cup trophy to win! The trophy was stolen while it was on display in a London museum. Luckily a British man was walking his dog in a London suburb a few months before the tournament was to begin. The dog started digging wildly in the ground and uncovered the trophy where someone had buried it. The Cup was back, and the games began shortly thereafter.

As it turned out, it may have been easier to find the lost Cup than to win it! England and West Germany each survived five matches to reach the final game. The 1966 Cup final was a classic battle between offense and defense. The West Germans had a powerful

Even the photographs can't say for sure! England's controversial third goal, scored by Geoffrey Hurst.

offense led by a 21-year-old halfback named Franz Beckenbauer. He was such a strong leader that he was known as "The Kaiser" (the German word for emperor).

On the other hand the British were known for their tough defense. They didn't score many goals, but they gave up even fewer. In the five games the English team had played to make it to the finals, they had given up just one goal. That goal was made by Eusebio of Portugal, one of the world's greatest scorers, on a penalty shot in the semifinals. England won that semifinal match, 2–1.

More than 100,000 noisy fans packed London's Wembley Stadium to watch the Cup final. The fans were especially excited. England was the country that had invented soccer, but this was the first time the English national team had ever reached the World Cup championship game.

West Germany scored within the first 10 minutes of the contest to take a 1–0 lead. The standing-room-only crowd in Wembley Stadium became a little nervous. Six minutes later, they felt much better when England's Geoffrey Hurst tied the score. The score remained 1–1 at the end of the first half.

One of the British team's mottos was "two goals and hold." They believed that if they could score one more time to make it 2–1, they could protect the lead with their great

defense and take home the world's most famous soccer trophy. England got its goal with only 12 minutes left in the match. The British fans began celebrating; they were confident their team would keep its lead and win the game.

Less than a minute remained in the contest when a British player committed a foul. That led to a free kick by the Germans that was blocked and then rebounded into the goal by Wolfgang Weber 15 seconds before regulation time ran out. For only the second time in World Cup history the final game would have to be decided in overtime.

In a soccer match overtime is not sudden death as it is in American football. Instead the teams play two 15-minute periods. The team that scores more often during overtime is the winner.

Ten minutes into the first overtime period the British went on an offensive attack. Nobby Stiles, the smallest man on the field, pushed the ball to his teammate Alan Ball. Ball noticed that Geoffrey Hurst was a step ahead of his West German defender and passed the ball to Hurst. Hurst raced in toward the goal and smashed the ball right at the German goalie.

German goalie Hans Tilkowski was in perfect position for the shot, but it came in a little higher than he expected. Tilkowski blocked the ball with his hands, it bounced high and behind him and kept moving toward the net. The ball hit the top crossbar of the net and dropped straight down. The question was, had the ball hit the ground behind the goal line—or right on the line? Remember, soccer rules say that the ball must land completely behind the goal line. No part of the ball can touch the line for a shot to count as a score.

The referee was not in the right spot to tell whether or not the shot was a goal. He asked the nearest linesman for his opinion, but the linesman's angle made it impossible for him to tell. It looked good to him, however, so he signaled a score. The British players and their fans cheered wildly and hugged each other. The West German players and coaches protested loudly. But the referee and linesman would not change their decision; England now led 3–2.

The West Germans began a wide open attack to try to tie the game before time ran out. They couldn't worry about defense. So when the British got control of the ball, they were able to charge the West German net and score again. The English defense held on for a 4–2 win.

The World Cup finally belonged to England. But the question remained: Was that first overtime shot really a goal? ★

DOWN BUT NOT OUT

T HAS BEEN MORE THAN 60 YEARS SINCE GENE Tunney fought Jack Dempsey for the heavyweight boxing championship. But there is still a debate about who really won that fight. It has gone down in sports history as "The Long Count."

The fight took place on September 22, 1927, at Chicago's Soldier's Field. Almost 105,000 boxing fans showed up to see Gene Tunney defend his heavyweight championship crown against Jack Dempsey. The fight was a rematch. One year before, Tunney had won the title from Dempsey. That first match hadn't even been close. Tunney had pounded his opponent for 10 rounds and had been named the winner by all three judges. Dempsey was determined to win back the crown that had once been his.

Before the fight the referee went over the rules with the two boxers. In the event of a knockdown, the referee said, the fighter still standing should go to the farthest neutral corner of the ring. A neutral corner was one in which neither of the fighters' trainers was standing. Only when a fighter reached the neutral corner would the referee begin the knockdown count.

There was a good reason for this rule. Suppose a fighter was knocked down but was able to get up before the count of 10. He should have at least a few seconds to get cleanly onto his feet before the fight continued. Otherwise, his opponent could continue pounding him and knock him down again before he stood up all the way.

For the first six rounds everything went smoothly. The fight was close, but Tunney seemed to be leading in the judges' scoring. Then in the seventh round, the two fighters closed in on each other. Tunney threw a hard punch with his left hand, and Dempsey countered with a long right. Tunney stepped back from that punch, but he wasn't prepared for the powerful left hook that followed. After Dempsey's blow connected, he followed with a series of lefts and rights. Suddenly Tunney went down.

It had all happened very quickly and unexpectedly. The huge crowd began yelling wildly. In all the excitement Dempsey forgot to go to the farthest neutral corner. Referee Dave Barry, who had begun counting to 10, stopped. He waved Dempsey away from the center of the ring where he was waiting to knock Tunney down again. Dempsey got the message, but he headed toward the nearest neutral corner, right behind Tunney. That was much too close as

far as the referee was concerned. He continued to wait.

All of this gave Tunney more time to regain his senses and his balance. At last Dempsey went to the correct corner, and the referee began the knockdown count. As the count reached four Tunney began getting up. Just as the referee was about to say, "Ten," Tunney was on his feet again. Realistically Tunney did not have 10 seconds to get up from the knockdown—he had closer to 15! The famous "Long Count" gave Tunney a chance to get back into the fight. Tunney had been down, but he was not out yet.

There were still almost two minutes left in the seventh round. Once he was on his feet Tunney began an attack of his own. By that point Dempsey was too exhausted and upset from his unsuccessful knockout to hold off the champ. Before the end of the round, Tunney landed a blow to Dempsey's chest that the challenger later said was the hardest punch he had ever felt.

Tunney kept up the attack for the final three rounds. He even knocked Dempsey down in the eighth round, though the challenger got right back up on his feet. When the bell sounded to end the 10th and final round, there was no question about the outcome of the fight. Gene Tunney had won, and he was still the heavyweight champion of the world.

Had Tunney really won the fight, or had he just gotten a lucky call from the referee? If Tunney had really needed 15 seconds to get up, then in a normal situation he would have been counted out and would have lost. Perhaps Tunney could have gotten up earlier, and he was just waiting for the count to reach nine before he did. If so, he probably would have won anyway. The debate about "The Long Count" has been going on for more than 60 years now.

Referee Dave Barry had his own opinion. "My impression of Tunney after he had been knocked down," he said, "was that he regained his senses in three or four seconds. Even if Dempsey had immediately retired to the neutral corner as instructed, Tunney would have been able to arise in good shape before the final count."

Interestingly enough, Jack Dempsey didn't talk about "The Long Count" when the fight was over and for all the years afterwards. He knew who was to blame for his losing his shot at the heavyweight crown, and he accepted that blame. ★

Jack Dempsey in a neutral corner and Gene Tunney on the canvas as the referee recites the knockdown count.

LEANING TO VICTORY

T TOOK JUST OVER 10 SECONDS TO COMPLETE THE 100-meter dash at the 1932 Olympic Games. But it took several hours to decide the winner. This was the first "photo finish" in Olympic history!

The winner of the men's 100-meter dash is often given the title, "the fastest man on earth." Two top runners from the U.S. were expected to put on a battle for that title at the 1932 Olympics. No one expected the battle to be as close as it was, however.

Eddie Tolan was America's top sprinter from 1929 to 1931. Ralph Metcalfe took over that Number 1 position during the early part of 1932. That made Metcalfe the favorite at the Olympics. But no one was counting Tolan out.

The two runners had very different styles, but both were effective. Tolan was short and relied on a quick start to get out front in a race. Then he would hold on to win. He often leaned into the tape at the finish line to get an extra edge.

etcalfe, who was much taller than Tolan, usually started off slowly. Then he would use his long stride to catch up to and go ahead of his competition near the end of the race.

The two men each won their semifinal heats in the Olympics to qualify for the finals. As they got set for the gold medal race, Tolan was in lane 1 and Metcalfe in lane 4.

As expected, Tolan got out of the blocks quickly and was the leader for the first 80 meters. Then Metcalfe caught him. They ran the final 10 meters absolutely even with one another. They broke the tape with their chests at exactly the same instant, with Tolan leaning forward and Metcalfe standing nearly straight up.

To the fans watching the race there seemed to be two possible results. One was that the athletes would share the gold medal. The other was that Metcalfe was the winner, since his final push put him slightly ahead

of Tolan just *after* the two men crossed the finish line.

The Olympic judges were not so sure. They called for photographs taken at the finish line to make the decision for them. The officials studied the photographs for several hours. They studied the Olympic rules as well. The rules said that the winner of a race "shall be the contestant whose torso is first over the finish line." The picture showed that by leaning in, Tolan's body had passed the finish line approximately *two inches* ahead of Metcalfe's. So Eddie Tolan was named the gold medalist.

What makes this story even more interesting is that if the same race occurred today Ralph Metcalfe would be declared the winner. Under today's rules, the winner is the person who reaches the finish line first, not who crosses it first. Ralph Metcalfe got to the line first, but Eddie Tolan leaned his torso across it for the victory.

There is another interesting story to tell about these two runners and the 1932 Olympics. The day after the 100-meter final, the 200-meter final was held. Once again Tolan and Metcalfe were the favorites. Tolan won again—this time by several feet. Metcalfe came in third behind another American, George Simpson. After the race, officials discovered that Metcalfe had been forced to start several feet behind where he should have. Because of that, he had actually run at least one meter farther than the other competitors. The officials offered to rerun the race, but Metcalfe refused. He didn't want to risk losing the one-two-three U.S. finish.

The 1932 Olympics just weren't lucky for Ralph Metcalfe. He had put on two gold medal performances, but he went home with a silver and a bronze medal instead. ★

Eddie Tolan (at bottom, with arms raised) posted a true photo-finish victory in the 1932 Olympic 100-meter dash. A hair's breadth behind was Ralph Metcalfe.